*The Psychology of the Esoteric*

Extemporaneous talks given by Osho in Mumbai, India

# OSHO

*The Psychology of the Esoteric*
*Insights into Energy and Consciousness*

Editing: Uti
Design: Soma
Typesetting: Soma
Production: Kamaal

Published by OSHO Media International,
17 Koregaon Park, Pune 411001 MS, India

Copyright © 1970, 2007 OSHO International Foundation,
www.osho.com/copyrights
Reprint 2011

All rights reserved. No part of this book may be reproduced or transmitted in any form or by any means, electronic or mechanical, including photocopying, recording, or by any information storage and retrieval system, without prior written permission from OSHO International Foundation.

OSHO is a registered trademark of OSHO International Foundation, used under license. www.osho.com/trademarks

Photos: Courtesy OSHO International Foundation

The material in this book is a transcript of a series of original OSHO Talks, *The Psychology of the Esoteric,* given to a live audience. All of Osho's talks have been published in full as books, and some are also available as original audio recordings. Audio recordings and the complete text archive can be found via the online OSHO Library at www.osho.com/library

Printed in India by Manipal Technologies Limited, Karnataka

ISBN 978-81-7261-211-5

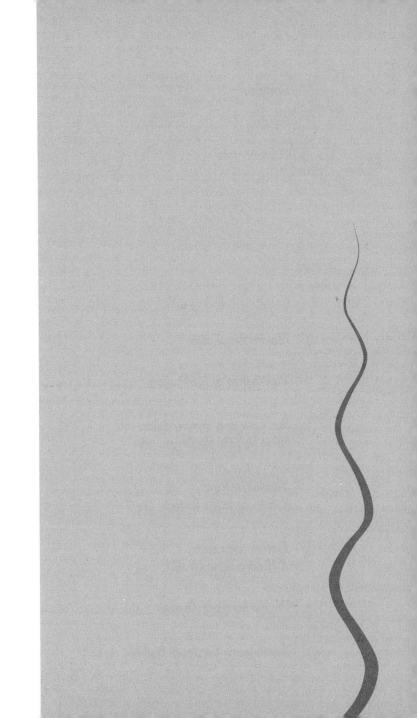

*Contents*

1/ *Inward Revolution*  1

2/ *The Mystery of Meditation*  17

3/ *Sex, Love and Prayerfulness:
Three Steps to the Divine*  39

4/ *Kundalini Yoga:
Returning to the Roots*  57

5/ *Esoteric Games:
A Hindrance to Growth*  85

6/ *The Psychology of Dreams*  105

7/ *Transcending the Seven Bodies*  129

8/ *Becoming and Being*   167

9/ *The Fallacy of Knowledge*   191

10/ *Truth, Goodness, Beauty:*
    *Windows to the Divine*   215

11/ *Right Questioning*   237

12/ *Balancing the Rational*
    *and the Irrational*   265

*About the Author*   298
*OSHO International Meditation Resort*   300
*More OSHO Books* 304
*For More Information*   308

*Preface*

**If esoteric work is introduced to you** without any foundation, you are not going to work for the foundation, because that is not interesting. The esoteric work is really very interesting, but I don't want you to make a temple without a foundation. It has happened many times; then the temple falls and destroys those who were building it.

The word *esoteric* simply means: you cannot put it objectively, scientifically. It is something inner, something subjective, something so mysterious, so miraculous that you can experience it but you cannot explain it. You can have it, but still you cannot explain it. It remains beyond explanation. And it is good that there is something in life which you cannot bring down to language, which you cannot bring down to the objective world – something which remains always beyond. You can become one with it.

I have been spontaneous in my work, but these are the mysteries of life, that existence itself has taken care. I have left it to existence, "Whatever you want me to do, I will do." I am not the doer; I am just a passage for existence to reach people. So I have never planned, but existence functions in a very planned way. So all the phases that have passed were necessary, and now we are ready to enter into the last phase – the ultimate ecstasy.

Ecstasy cannot be pragmatic.

Love cannot be pragmatic.

Trust cannot be pragmatic.

All that is valuable is esoteric.

Osho, *Beyond Psychology*

# I / *Inward Revolution*

*Osho,
On man's path of evolution, is it possible that at some time in the future humanity as a whole can attain enlightenment? At what point of evolution is man today?*

**With man, the natural,** automatic process of evolution ends. Man is the last product of unconscious evolution. With man, conscious evolution begins. Many things are to be taken into account.

First, unconscious evolution is mechanical and natural. It happens by itself. Through this type of evolution, consciousness evolves. But the moment consciousness comes into being, unconscious evolution stops because its purpose has been fulfilled. Unconscious evolution is needed only up to the point where the conscious comes into being. Man has become conscious. In a way, he has transcended nature. Now nature cannot do anything; the last product that was possible through natural evolution has come into being. Now man becomes free to decide whether to evolve or not to evolve.

Secondly, unconscious evolution is collective, but the moment evolution becomes conscious it becomes individual. No collective, automatic evolution proceeds further than mankind. From now on, evolution becomes an individual process. Consciousness creates individuality. Before consciousness evolves, there is no individuality; only species exist, not individuality.

When evolution is still unconscious, it is an automatic process; there is no uncertainty about it. Things happen through the law of cause and effect. Existence is mechanical and certain. But with man, with consciousness, uncertainty comes into existence. Now nothing is certain. Evolution may take place or it may not. The potential is there, but the choice will rest entirely with each individual. That is why anxiety is a human phenomenon. Below man there is no anxiety because there is no choice. Everything happens as it must. There is no choice so there is no chooser, and in the absence of the chooser, anxiety is impossible. *Who* is to be anxious? *Who* is to be tense?

With the possibility of choice, anxiety follows like a shadow. Now everything has to be chosen; everything is a conscious effort. You alone are responsible. If you fail, you fail. It is your responsibility. If you succeed, you succeed. It is again your responsibility. And every choice is ultimate in a sense. You cannot undo it, you cannot forget it, you cannot go back on it. Your choice becomes your destiny. It will remain with you and be a part of you; you cannot deny it. But your choice is always a gamble. Every choice is made in darkness because nothing is certain.

That is why man suffers from anxiety. He is anxious to his very roots. What torments him, to begin with, is: To be or not to be? To do or not to do? To do this or to do that? "No choice" is not possible. If you do not choose, then you are choosing not to choose; it is a choice. So you are forced to choose; you are not free not to choose. Not choosing will have as much effect as any other choice.

The dignity, the beauty and the glory of man is this consciousness. But it is a burden also. The glory and the burden come simultaneously the minute you become conscious. Every step is a movement between the two. With man, choice and conscious individuality come into existence. You can evolve, but your evolution will be an individual endeavor. You may evolve to become a buddha or you may not. The choice is yours.

So there are two types of evolution: collective evolution and individual, conscious evolution. *Evolution* implies unconscious, collective progress, so it would be better to use the word *revolution* in talking about man. With man, revolution becomes possible.

*Revolution*, as I am using the word here, means a conscious, individual effort toward evolution. It is bringing individual responsibility to a peak. Only you are responsible for your own evolution. Ordinarily, man tries to escape from his responsibility for his own evolution, from the responsibility of freedom of choice. There is a great fear of freedom. When you are a slave the responsibility for your life is never yours; someone else is responsible. So in a way, slavery is a very comfortable thing. There is no burden. In this respect, slavery is a freedom: freedom from conscious choice.

## Inward Revolution

The moment you become completely free, you have to make your own choices. No one forces you to do anything; all alternatives are open to you. Then the struggle with the mind begins. So one becomes afraid of freedom.

Part of the appeal of ideologies such as communism and fascism is that they provide an escape from individual freedom and a shirking of individual responsibility. The burden of responsibility is taken away from the individual; the society becomes responsible. When something goes wrong, you can always point to the state, the organization. Man becomes just a part of the collective structure. But in denying individual freedom, fascism and communism also deny the possibility of human evolution. It is a falling back from the great possibility that revolution offers: the total transformation of human beings. When this happens, you destroy the possibility of achieving the ultimate. You fall back; you again become like animals.

To me, further evolution is possible only with individual responsibility. You alone are responsible! This responsibility is a great blessing in disguise. With this individual responsibility comes the struggle that ultimately leads to choiceless awareness.

The old pattern of unconscious evolution has ended for us. You can fall back into it, but you cannot remain in it. Your being will revolt. Man has become conscious; he has to remain conscious. There is no other way.

Philosophers like Aurobindo have great appeal for escapists. They say that collective evolution is possible. The divine will descend and everyone will become enlightened. But to me that is not possible. And even if it appears possible, it is not worthwhile. If you become enlightened without your own individual effort, then that enlightenment is not worth having. It will not give you the ecstasy that crowns the effort. It will just be taken for granted – like your eyes, your hands, your breathing system. These are great blessings, but no one really values them, cherishes them.

If one day you could also be born with enlightenment, just as Aurobindo promises, it would be valueless. You would have much, but because it had come to you without effort, without toil, it would mean nothing to you; its significance would be lost. Conscious effort is necessary. The achievement is not as significant as the effort itself. Effort gives it its meaning, struggle gives it its significance.

As I see it, enlightenment that comes collectively, unconsciously, as a gift from the divine, is not only impossible but also meaningless. You must struggle for enlightenment. Through struggle, you create the capacity to see and feel and hold on to the bliss that comes.

Unconscious evolution ends with man, and conscious evolution – revolution – begins. But conscious evolution does not necessarily begin in any particular man. It begins only if you choose it to begin. If you do not choose it – as most people do not – you will be in a very tense condition. And present-day humanity is like this: nowhere to go, nothing to be achieved. Nothing can be achieved now without conscious effort. You cannot go back to a state of unconsciousness. The door has closed; the bridge has been broken.

The conscious choice to evolve is a great adventure, the only adventure there is for a human being. The path is arduous; it is bound to be so. Errors are bound to be there, failures, because nothing is certain. This situation creates tension in the mind. You do not know where you are, you do not know

## Inward Revolution

where you are going. Your identity is lost. The situation may even reach such a point that you become suicidal.

Suicide is a human phenomenon; it comes with human choice. Animals cannot commit suicide, because to choose death consciously is impossible for them. Birth is unconscious, death is unconscious. But with man — ignorant man, unevolved man — one thing becomes possible: the ability to choose death. Your birth is not your choice. As far as your birth is concerned, you are in the hands of unconscious evolution. In fact, your birth is not a human happening at all. It is animal in nature, because it is not your choice. Only with choice does humanity begin. But you can choose your death — a decisive act. So suicide becomes a definite human act. And if you do not choose conscious evolution, there is every possibility that you may choose to commit suicide. You may not have the courage to actively commit suicide but you will go through a slow, prolonged process of suicide — lingering, waiting to die.

You cannot make anyone else responsible for your evolution. To accept this situation gives you strength. You are on your way to growing, to evolving. We create gods, or we take refuge in gurus, so that we will not have to be responsible for our own lives, for our own evolution. We try to place the responsibility somewhere else, away from us. If we are not able to accept some god or some guru, then we try to escape from responsibility through intoxicants or drugs, through anything that will make us unconscious. But these efforts to deny responsibility are absurd, juvenile, childish. They only postpone the problem; they are not solutions. You can postpone until death, but the problem still remains, and your new birth will continue in the same way.

Once you become aware that you alone are responsible, there is no escape through any type of unconsciousness. And you are foolish if you try to escape, because responsibility is a great opportunity for evolution. Out of the struggle that is created, something new may evolve. To become aware means to know that everything depends on you. Even your god depends on you, because he is created by your imagination.

Everything is ultimately a part of you, and you are responsible for it. There is no one to listen to your excuses; there are no courts of appeal, the whole responsibility is yours. You are alone, absolutely alone. This has to be understood very clearly. The moment a person becomes conscious, he becomes alone. The greater the consciousness, the greater the awareness that you are alone. So, do not escape from this fact through society, friends, associations, crowds. Do not escape from it! It is a great phenomenon; the whole process of evolution has been working toward this.

Consciousness has come to the point now where you know that you are alone. And only in aloneness can you attain enlightenment. I am not saying *loneliness*. The feeling of loneliness is the feeling that comes when one is escaping from aloneness, when one is not ready to accept it. If you do not accept the fact of aloneness, then you will feel lonely. Then you will find some crowd or some means of intoxication in which to forget yourself. Loneliness will create its own magic of forgetfulness. If you can be alone even for a single moment, totally alone, the ego will die; the "I" will die. You will explode; you will be no more. The ego cannot remain alone. It can exist only in relation to others. Whenever you are alone, a miracle happens. The ego becomes weak. Now it cannot continue to exist for long. So if you can be courageous enough to be alone, you will gradually become egoless.

To be alone is a very conscious and deliberate act, more deliberate than suicide, because the ego cannot exist alone, but it can exist in suicide. Egoistic people are more prone to suicide. Suicide is always in relation to someone else; it is never an act of aloneness. In suicide, the ego will not suffer. Rather, it will become more expressive. It will enter into a new birth with greater force.

Through aloneness, the ego is shattered. It has nothing to relate to, so it cannot exist. So, if you are ready to be alone, unwaveringly alone, neither escaping nor falling back, just accepting the fact of aloneness as it is, it becomes a great opportunity. Then you are just like a seed that has much potential in it. But remember, the seed must destroy itself for the plant to grow. Ego is a seed, a potentiality. If it is shattered, the divine is born. The divine is neither "I" nor "thou," it is *one*. Through aloneness, you come to this oneness.

You can create false substitutes for this oneness. Hindus become one, Christians become one, Mohammedans become one; India is one, China is one. These are just substitutes for oneness. Oneness comes only through total aloneness.

A crowd can call itself one, but the oneness is always in opposition to something else. Since the crowd is with you, you are at ease. Now you are not responsible any more. You would not burn a mosque alone, you would not destroy a temple alone, but as part of a crowd you can do it, because now you are not individually responsible. Everyone is responsible, so no one in particular is responsible. There is no individual consciousness, only a group consciousness. You regress in a crowd and become like an animal.

The crowd is a false substitute for the feeling of oneness. One who is aware of the situation, aware of his responsibility as a human being, aware of the difficult, arduous task that comes with being human, does not choose any false substitutes. He lives with the facts as they are; he does not create any fictions. Your religions and your political ideologies are just fictions, creating an illusory feeling of oneness.

Oneness comes only when you become egoless, and the ego can die only when you are totally alone. When you are completely alone, you are not. That very moment is the moment of explosion. You explode into the infinite. This, and only this, is evolution. I call it revolution because it is not unconscious. You may become egoless or you may not. It is up to you. To be alone is the only real revolution. Much courage is needed.

Only a Buddha is alone, only a Jesus or a Mahavira is alone. It is not that they left their families, left the world. It looks that way, but it is not. They were not negatively leaving something. The act was positive; it was a movement toward aloneness. They were not leaving. They were in search of being totally alone. The whole search is for that moment of explosion when one is alone. In aloneness there is bliss. And only then is enlightenment achieved. We cannot be alone, others also cannot be alone, so we create groups, families, societies, nations. All nations, all families, all groups are made up of cowards, of those who are not courageous enough to be alone.

Real courage is the courage to be alone. It means a conscious realization of the fact that you *are* alone and you cannot be otherwise. You can either deceive yourself or you can live with this fact. You can continue deceiving yourself for lives

## Inward Revolution

and lives, but you will just go on in a vicious circle. Only if you can live with this fact of aloneness is the circle broken and you come to the center. That center is the center of divineness, of the whole, the holy. I cannot conceive of a time when every human being will be able to achieve this as a birthright. It is impossible.

Consciousness is individual. Only unconsciousness is collective. Human beings have come to the point of consciousness where they have become individuals. There is no humanity as such; there are only individual human beings. Each human being must realize his own individuality and the responsibility for it. The first thing we must do is to accept aloneness as a basic fact and learn to live with it. We must not create any fictions. If you create fictions you will never be able to know the truth. Fictions are projected, created, cultivated truths that prevent you from knowing what is. Live with the fact of your aloneness. If you can live with this fact, if there is no fiction between you and this fact, then the truth will be revealed to you. Every fact, if looked into deeply, reveals the truth.

So live with the fact of responsibility, with the fact that you are alone. If you can live with this fact, the explosion will happen. It is arduous, but it is the only way. Through difficulty, through accepting this truth, you reach the point of explosion. Only then is there bliss. If it is given to you ready-made, it loses its worth because you have not earned it. You do not have the capacity to feel the bliss. This capacity comes only from discipline.

If you can live with the fact of your responsibility for yourself, a discipline will automatically come to you. By being totally responsible for yourself, you cannot help but become disciplined. But this discipline is not something forced upon you from the outside. It comes from within. Because of the total responsibility you carry for yourself, each step you take is disciplined. You cannot utter even one word irresponsibly. If you are aware of your own aloneness, you will be aware of the anguish of others also. Then you will not be able to commit a single irresponsible act, because you will feel responsible not only for yourself but for others also. If you can live with the fact of your aloneness, you know that everyone is lonely. Then the son knows that the father is lonely; the wife knows that the husband is lonely; the husband knows that the wife is lonely. Once you know this, it is impossible not to be compassionate.

Living with facts is the only yoga, the only discipline. Once you are totally aware of the human situation, you become religious. You become a master of yourself. But the austerity that comes is not the austerity of an ascetic. It is not forced; it is not ugly. The austerity is aesthetic. You feel that it is the only thing possible, that you cannot do otherwise. Then you renounce things; you become non-possessive.

The urge to possess is the urge not to be alone. One cannot be alone, so he seeks company. But the company of other people is not reliable, so he seeks, instead, the company of things. To live with a wife is difficult; to live with a car is not so difficult. So ultimately, possessiveness turns toward things.

You may even try to change persons into things. You try to mold them in such a way that they lose their personalities, their individuality. A wife is a thing, not a person; a husband is a thing, not a person.

If you become aware of your aloneness, then you become aware of the aloneness of others also. Then you know that to try to possess another is trespassing. You never positively renounce. Renunciation becomes the negative shadow of your aloneness; you become non-possessive. Then you can be a lover, but not a husband, not a wife.

With this non-possessiveness comes compassion and austerity. Innocence comes to you. When you deny the facts of life, you cannot be innocent; you become cunning. You deceive yourself and others. But if you are courageous enough to live with the facts as they are, you become innocent. This innocence is not cultivated. You are it: innocent.

To me, to be innocent is all that is to be achieved. Be innocent, and the divine is always blissfully flowing toward you. Innocence is the capacity to receive, to be part of the divine. Be innocent, and the guest is there. Become the host.

This innocence cannot be cultivated because cultivation is always a contrivance. It is calculated. But innocence can never be calculated; it is impossible.

Innocence is religiousness. To be innocent is the peak of true realization. But true innocence comes only through a conscious revolution; it is not possible through any collective, unconscious evolution. Man is alone. He is free to choose heaven or hell, life or death, the ecstasy of realization or the misery of our so-called life.

Sartre said somewhere: "Man is condemned to be free." You may choose either heaven or hell. Freedom means the freedom to choose either. If you can choose only heaven, then it is not a choice; it is not freedom. Heaven without the choice of hell will be hell itself. Choice always means either/or. It does not mean you are free to choose only good. Then there would be no freedom.

If you choose wrongly, freedom becomes a condemnation; but if you choose rightly, it becomes bliss. It depends on you whether your choice turns your freedom into condemnation or into bliss. The choice is totally your responsibility.

If you are ready, then from within your depths a new dimension can begin: the dimension of revolution. Evolution has ended. Now a revolution is needed to open you up to what is beyond. It is an individual revolution, an inward revolution.

# 2/ *The Mystery of Meditation*

*Osho,*
*I have been going around in a circle, and feel in some ways I have completed the circle, but in other ways I am stuck on the circumference. Do you have any program, or some point of meditation, or point of enabling one to come to meditation, that you suggest at the beginning?*

**Meditation is not only a method;** it is not simply a technique. You cannot learn it. It is a growth — a growth of your total living, out of your total living. Meditation is not something which can be added to you as you are. It cannot be added to you; it can come out of you through a basic transformation, through a mutation.

Ordinarily meditation is understood as a technique which can be added to a person. To me it is not so. As you are, meditation cannot be added

## The Mystery of Meditation

to you. Meditation is a flowering, it is a growth. And growth is always out of the total. It is not an addition; just like love, it cannot be added to you. It is a growth out of you, of your totality. So you can *grow* toward meditation.

So first, this total flowering of personality must be understood correctly. Otherwise one can play with mental tricks and there are so many. For some time you will be befooled by the tricks. But it's not only that you are befooled. In a real sense, not only do you not gain anything out of it, you are harmed also, because the very attitude – to think of meditation in terms of method – is basically wrong. And when one begins to play with mental tricks, the quality of the mind deteriorates. As mind exists, it is not meditative. So the total mind must change before meditation can come in. What is the mind as it is? How does it function?

It functions anti-meditatively.

First, the mind is always verbalizing. It is verbal, and the verbalizing is taken as thinking. It is not. You can know words, you can know language, you can know the conceptual structure of thinking, but it is not thinking. On the contrary, it is to escape from thinking. You see a flower and you verbalize it; you see a man passing and you verbalize it. Every situation is verbalized. The mind has become only a verbalizing mechanism. It can translate every existential thing into a word – everything is being transformed constantly into words. These words create a barrier, these words become the imprisonment. These words – this constant flow, transformation of things into words, of existence into words – is the barrier, is the obstacle toward the meditative mind.

So the first requirement toward meditative growth is to be aware of this constant verbalizing and to be able to stop it.

Just see things; don't verbalize. Be aware of their presence but don't change them into words. Live with things without language; with people without language; with situations without language. This is not impossible. This is natural and possible. Every situation is artificial, a created situation, and we have become so mechanically habituated to it that we are never aware of the transformation of the translation.

There is a sunrise. You are never aware of the gap – you see it, you feel it and you verbalize it. But the gap is never felt – the gap between the feeling and the verbalizing. In that gap, in that interval, one must become aware. One must become aware of the fact that sunrise as such is not a word; it is a fact, a presence, a situation. The mind automatically changes it into a word. These words are accumulated. They go on being accumulated and between existence, the existential and consciousness, these piled up words – these piled up memories, linguistic memories – these are the obstacles toward meditative growth.

Meditation means living in a situation without words, living in a situation non-linguistically. Sometimes it happens spontaneously also. When you are in love with someone, the non-linguistic moment is prolonged. If you are really in love then presence is felt, and language is not. So whenever two lovers are in intimate relationship they become silent. It is not that there is nothing to express. On the contrary, much is overwhelming them, wanting to be expressed. But words are not there; they cannot be. They only come when the love has gone.

If two lovers are not silent and are talking, that is an indication that the love has died. Now they are filling the gap with words. When love is living, words are not, because the very existence of love is so overwhelming, so penetrating,

## The Mystery of Meditation

that the barrier is crossed – the barrier of language and words. And ordinarily only in love is the barrier crossed.

That's why prayerfulness is a further step of love, and meditation is the culmination, the culmination of love: love, not with a single person – with an individual – but with the total existence. So to me, meditation is a loving relationship with the total existence, with all that surrounds you. If you can be in a love situation with it, then you are in meditation.

And this is not a mental trick. This is not "making" the mind still; rather it is understanding the mechanism of the mind. It is not interfering with the mechanism; rather it is a deep understanding of the total mechanism of the mind. The moment you understand your mechanical habit of verbalization, of verbalizing, the mechanical habit of changing things and existence into words, the moment you understand it, the gap is there. It comes spontaneously. It follows understanding. It is just like a shadow of the understanding.

So, first one has to understand how one is *not* in meditation. The real problem is not how to meditate; the real problem is to know why we are not in meditation. The real problem is not how to love, but to know why we are not in love. It is negative; the real process of meditation is negative. It is not adding something positively to you, but rather, on the contrary, negating something from you, which has already been added to you.

The society gives language; the society cannot exist without language. Human society is an outgrowth of language; there are no animal societies because they have no language. Language creates the society. Society needs language; existence doesn't need it. Existence can be without language; society cannot be. So I am not saying that you must be without language – you will have to be with language. But this mechanism must be a mechanism which can be put on and off.

When you are a social being the mechanism must be on: the mechanism of language. Without this you cannot exist within society. But when you are with existence, the mechanism must be turned off – and you must be able to put it off, otherwise the mechanism is mad. If you cannot turn it off – and it goes on and on, and you are not capable of putting it off, then the mechanism has taken hold over you – then you have become just a slave to the mechanism, to the instrument. Mind must be used as an instrument, and not as a master. It has become the master.

Mind as master is the non-meditative state. You, the consciousness as the master, is the meditative state. So meditation is mastering the mechanism, the mind.

The linguistic function of the mind is not the all and end all. You are behind it and existence is beyond it. Consciousness is behind the linguistic mechanism and existence is beyond the linguistic mechanism. And when consciousness and existence are in communion, that state I call meditation – consciousness and existence in communion.

So language must be dropped. When I say "must be dropped" I don't mean that you must push it away, you must suppress it, you must cut it away – I don't mean that. What I mean is: you must understand that a habit which is needed in society has become a habit of twenty-four hours, which is not needed. When you walk, you need legs to move. They should not move when you are sitting. When you are sitting, if your legs go on moving then you are mad; then the legs have gone insane. You must be able to turn them off. When you are not talking with somebody, then language must not be there.

## The Mystery of Meditation

It is a talking instrument, a technique to communicate. When you are communicating something, language should be used. But when you are not communicating with somebody, language should not be there.

If you are able – and you can be by understanding – then you can *grow* into meditation. I say you can "grow" because alive processes are never dead additions. They are always growing processes. So meditation is a process, not a technique. Technique is always dead – it can be added. Process is always living – it grows and widens.

So the first thing: language is needed, it is necessary, but you must not always remain in it. There must be moments when you are existential and not linguistic, when you just exist. It will not be just vegetating because consciousness is there, and it is more acute, and it is more living, because language dulls the consciousness.

Language is bound to be repetitive. Language is *bound* to be repetitive. Existence is never repetitive. So, through language comes boredom, and the more powerful language becomes – the more the mind becomes linguistically oriented – the more bored it is, because language is a repetition. Existence is not.

When you see a rose, it is not a repetition. It is a new rose, altogether new. It has never been and it will never be again. For the first time and the last time it is there. But when you say "this is a rose," this word *rose* is a repetition. It has always been there; it will always be there. You have killed the new through the old word.

Existence is always young, language is always old. And through language, you escape existence. In fact through language you escape life, because language is dead. And the more you are involved in it, the more you are in it, you are being deadened by it. So if you have to find a person who is completely dead, you will have to find a pundit. A pundit is completely dead because he is language, words and nothing else.

Sartre has given his autobiography the name *Words*. It is the autobiography of everyone more or less. We live in words. That is, we don't live. And in the end there is only a series of words accumulated and nothing else. Words are like still thoughts. You see something, you take a picture; the picture is dead. The situation is never dead. Then you can make an album of dead pictures. In the end, a person who has not been in meditation is just like a dead album: only linguistic pictures, memories. Nothing lived, everything verbalized.

Meditation means living, living totally, and you can live totally only when the barrier of language is crossed, when you are silent. But by being silent, I don't mean unconscious. You can be silent and unconscious, then it is not a living silence. Again, you have escaped.

So through a mantra you can autohypnotize yourself. By simply repeating a word you can create so much boredom for your mind that it goes to sleep. Boredom is a necessary step toward sleep. You just drop into sleep, in the unconscious. So, so many – rather *all* techniques of meditation – are techniques toward boredom, or they are autohypnotic. You can go on chanting "Ram, Ram, Ram." The mind will feel bored, will feel sleepy. And if you go on chanting and chanting, then it will go to sleep. Then language will not be there, the linguistic barrier will not be there, but you will be unconscious.

Meditation means language should not be there, and you should be conscious. Otherwise there is no communion with existence, with all that exists, with all that is. What can be done?

## The Mystery of Meditation

No mantra can help, no chanting can help. They cannot be instrumental to meditation. They can only be instrumental toward autohypnosis, and autohypnosis is not meditation. It is quite the contrary. To be in an autohypnotized state is regression. It is not going beyond language; it is falling below it.

So what can be done? In fact, you cannot do anything except understand, because whatsoever you can do will come out of *you*. And you are confused, and you are not in meditation, and your mind is not silent. So anything out of you will create more confusion. All that can be done is to understand.

Begin to understand how the mind has taken complete charge of you, and let there be moments, allow moments, when words are not. You cannot push away words because even the very pushing away will take linguistic forms. If you want to push away words, you will push them with other words. And then a vicious circle is created. You cannot push away words through words. That is impossible, because by using words to push, you are still using language and strengthening the barrier. So no word can be used; that means no mantra can be used. You have just to be aware of how the mind functions, because awareness is not a word. It is an act – existential, not mental. An existential act, any existential act, will be a help.

And the first existential act that can be used is awareness. Be aware of your mental processes, how your mind works. The moment you become aware of the function of the mind, you are not mind. The very awareness of mental processes means you are beyond: aloof, a witness. And the more you become aware, the more you become able to see the gaps: the gaps are there, but you are so unaware that they are never seen and perceived. The gaps are always there. Between two words there is always a gap. Otherwise the two words cannot remain two. They will become one.

Between two words there is always a gap, howsoever unperceivable, howsoever small, but the gap is there. Between two notes of music there is silence, howsoever small, howsoever unperceivable. Otherwise two notes cannot be two; two words cannot be two without the interval – a wordless interval is always there. But one has to be keenly aware, attentive, to know the gap, the interval.

The more you become aware, the slower the mind goes. It is always relative. The less you are aware, the faster the mind is; the more you are aware, the slower the process of the mind is. With all things…but because you have become aware, it looks slower, it *appears* slower; it is the same. But you are keen, you are observing, you have become more conscious. More consciousness means a slower mind. When the mind is slower, gaps widen; you can perceive them.

It is just like a film. If a projector is run slowly, then you see the gaps. There are so many gaps – gaps and gaps and gaps. If I raise my hand, it cannot be filmed without gaps. I can raise it without gaps, but it can never be filmed without gaps. My hand raised, one foot raised, will have to be shot in a thousand parts and each part will be a still, dead photograph. These thousand parts, part-photographs – partial, dead – if they can be passed before your eyes so fast that you cannot see the gap, then you see the hand raised. Then you see the hand raised as a process because the gaps are not seen. Otherwise, films can never be taken without gaps. The gaps are there.

Mind, too, is just like a projector, a linguistic projector. Gaps are there. Be more aware and attentive of your mind,

## The Mystery of Meditation

and you will see the gaps. It is just like a gestalt picture. A picture can be made which can be seen as two things, but you cannot see the two things simultaneously. The picture can be of an old lady, and the same picture can be of a younger one. Both are in the picture but if you see one, you will not see the other because the attention changes. You are focused on one, then the other is not seen. When you see the other, the previous one is lost.

Now you know that the same dots, the same inkblot, has two pictures. Now you know perfectly well, you have seen both, but you cannot see both simultaneously. Still, you cannot see both simultaneously. If you see the old lady, the younger is not seen. And you will even have some difficulty to change from one picture to another, because the focus becomes focused. You know – now you have seen the other picture also – but you will have some difficulty to change the focus. When the focus is changed the younger lady will be seen, but the older one will be lost.

The same thing happens with the mind also. It is a gestalt. If you see the words, you cannot see the gaps. If you see the gaps, you cannot see the words. But now you know: there are words and there are gaps, and every word is followed by a gap and every gap is followed by a word, but you cannot see both simultaneously. If you are focused on the gap, words will be lost and you will be thrown into meditation. Words will not be there. The gap!

These words and these gaps, these are two things in the mind. Mind is divided into two things – gaps and words – but every word follows a gap and every gap follows a word. The division is in a series; the mind is not divided into two watertight compartments – words and gaps. They are mixed.

They are in a chain. Two words are being connected through a gap, and two gaps are being connected through a word.

Mind focused, consciousness focused, only on words is non-meditative. Consciousness focused only on gaps is meditative. So meditation is a "gestalt attention" – attention, awareness, consciousness of the gaps. And you cannot be simultaneously aware of both, that is impossible. So, whenever you become aware, words will be lost. When you observe keenly, you will not find words; you will find only the gap.

Not even "gaps" because you can feel the difference between two words, but you cannot feel the difference between two gaps. So words are always plural and gap is always singular: the gap. That's why I use "the gap." Words can be many; gaps cannot be. They become one. They trespass and they become one. So meditation to me means focusing on the gap. The gestalt is to be changed, and the gestalt changes…the gestalt changes.

Another thing is to be understood. If you have the gestalt picture and if you concentrate on the figure of the old lady, you don't know the other picture. You have become conscious of the one, and that's the only way. You become conscious of one. You don't know that the other picture is hiding behind it. You have become conscious of one. If you concentrate on the picture of the old lady – if you go on concentrating and focusing, if you become totally attentive to it – a moment will come and the focus will have changed. The old lady is gone, and now you see the other picture. The other picture comes in.

Why does it happen? It happens because the mind cannot be focused continuously for a long time. It has to change, it has to change. Either it will have to go to sleep or it will have to change. There are only two possibilities. If you go on

## The Mystery of Meditation

concentrating, centering your consciousness on the figure of the old lady, either you will go to sleep... That is meditation Mahesh Yogi style – you will go to sleep. It is peaceful, it is vital, it is a refreshment. You come out of it refreshed. It can help physical health, it can help a mental equilibrium also, but it is not meditation.

The same can be done by autohypnosis, by suggestion – by Coué also – the same can be done. To take it as meditation is very dangerous; it is not. And if one thinks of it as meditation then he will never search for the real dimension of meditation. That is the real harm done by such practices, and by the propagandists of such practices. It is drugging yourself psychologically.

The mind cannot remain in a fixed position. It is a living process. It cannot remain in a fixed position. If you force it to then it will go to sleep only in order to continue the living process in dreams. It goes to sleep only in order to escape your stagnant, forceful focus. Then it can again continue living in dreams.

If you are aware – only aware, without words – then autohypnosis becomes difficult. Without words, autohypnosis is difficult, because without words you cannot suggest anything to the mind. The Indian word *mantra* means suggestion, and nothing else. It means suggestion. If you are simply aware, without words, of the old lady and her figure, then you will see that your mind changes, the focus changes, and the younger woman comes into focus.

Why I'm saying this...if you become aware of words – just become aware of words and don't use any word to push them away, don't use any mantra to push them away, just become aware of the words – your mind will change automatically to gaps. It cannot continue. It will have to relax into the gap.

Either you are identified with words...then you go on jumping from one word to another. You escape the gap and go on jumping from one word to another, because another word is also something new. You have changed the word: the older word is not there and the newer word is there, so the mind goes on changing, the focus is changing.

Or, if you are not identified with words, if you are just a witness, just seeing words in a procession, just watching, aloof, just standing above and looking at the words...they are going in a procession, just like the street traffic goes, and you are just looking at it; things are changing, one person has passed, another has not yet come... There is a gap; the street is vacant.

If you are just watching, then you will know the gap. And once you have known the gap, you will know the jump, because the gap is the abyss. The word is the surface and the gap is the abyss. Once you have known the gap you are in it, you will jump into it, and it is so peace-giving, and it is so consciousness-creating. It is a mutation to be in the gap; it is a transformation to be in the gap. And once you have known the treasure of the gap, you will not lose it.

The moment language is not needed, you will drop it – and it is a conscious dropping. You are conscious of the abyss, you are conscious of the silence, the infinite silence. You are in it.

And another thing: when you are in the gap, in the interval, in the abyss, you become one with it. You cannot be separate from it. You are conscious and one, and that is the mystery of meditation. You are perfectly conscious and one with it also. It is not that you are conscious of something else separate from you – the other. You are never conscious of the abyss as the other; you are conscious of the abyss as yourself. And still you are conscious; you are not unconscious. You know, but the

## The Mystery of Meditation

knower is now the knowing. You observe the gap, but now the observer is the observed.

Now as far as words and thoughts are concerned, you are a witness, separate, and words are the other. But when there are no words, you are the gap, and still conscious that you are the gap – because now between you and the gap, between consciousness and existence, there is no barrier. Only words are the barrier. Now you are in an existential situation. This is meditation: to be in existence, totally in it and still conscious. And this is the contradiction, and this is the paradox, because we have never known a situation in which we are conscious and one with it.

Whenever we are conscious of anything, the thing becomes the other. If we are identified we know only one thing. Then the thing is not the other, but then we are not conscious. We can be one with something only when we are unconscious. That has been our experience. That is the ordinary experience, the day-to-day experience: we become one only when we are unconscious.

That's why sex has got so much appeal. You become one in a moment, but in that moment you are unconscious, and you seek that unconsciousness. But the more you seek, the more conscious you become. Then sex becomes absolutely absurd. A moment will come…because if you practice this continuously you cannot remain unconscious. Consciousness will penetrate into it. The thing will become mechanical, because then you cannot be identified with it. Then you cannot feel the bliss of sex, because the bliss was coming from the unconscious – you could become unconscious in a passionate thrill.

Your consciousness was dropped for a single moment; you were in the abyss but unconscious. But the moment you go into it, the small becomes the moment. And the more you seek it, the more it is lost. And a moment comes when you are in sex and not unconscious. The abyss is lost, the bliss is lost. Then the act becomes stupid. Then the act becomes just a mechanical relief; then there is no spiritual background to it.

We have only known unconscious oneness; we have never known conscious oneness – and meditation is conscious oneness. It is the other pole of sexuality. Sex is one pole of unconscious oneness, and meditation is the other pole, of conscious oneness. Sex is the lowest point of oneness and meditation is the peak, the highest peak of oneness. And the difference is of consciousness. The difference is of consciousness.

The Western mind is thinking about meditation because the appeal of sex has been lost. Whenever a society becomes unsuppressively sexual, meditation will follow. Whenever a society is uninhibitedly sexual, meditation will follow – because uninhibited sex will kill the charm and the romance, will kill the spiritual side. You cannot be so unconscious. You cannot be unconscious so often. Otherwise the very unconsciousness will have a conscious corner.

So a sexually suppressed society can remain interested in sex, but the unsuppressive, non-suppressive, uninhibited society cannot remain in sexuality forever. It will have to transcend it. So whenever sex becomes free, uninhibited, meditation follows. And whenever a society is sexual, religion will follow. A sexually suppressive society cannot be really religious because the function of meditation is being substituted by sex. So to me, a sexually free society is a step toward a religious revolution. The Western mind is asking "What is meditation?" – a seeking, a searching. And the search will become keener as days pass.

## The Mystery of Meditation

Of course, because the search is there, it can be exploited. And it is being exploited by the East. It can be exploited. Gurus can be supplied; they can be exported, and they *are* being exported. But only tricks can be found through gurus – only tricks. Understanding comes through life, understanding comes through living. It cannot be given and transferred.

I cannot give you my understanding. I can talk about it, but I cannot give it to you. You will have to find it. You will have to go into life. You will have to err, you will have to fail, you will have to pass through frustration. And only through failures, errors, frustrations, through the encounter of real living, will you come to meditation. That's why I say it is a growth. But something can be understood. The understanding will never be deeper than intellect. Through another it can never be more than intellectual.

That's why Krishnamurti demands the impossible. He will say to you, "Don't understand me intellectually." But through another, nothing except intellectual understanding can come. That's why his effort has been absurd. Whatsoever he is saying is exactly what can be said; it is authentic. But when he demands more than intellectual understanding from the listener, it becomes impossible, because through another nothing more can come out…nothing more can be delivered. But to me, even intellectual understanding is worthwhile.

If you can understand what I say intellectually, you can also understand what has not been said to you. If you can understand what I am saying to you, you can also understand the gaps: what I am not saying to you, what I cannot say to you. And if you understand intellectually…and first understanding is bound to be intellectual, because intellect is the door. It can never be spiritual, because spirituality is the inner shrine.

So I can only communicate to you intellectually. But if you understand it, then that which has not been said can also be felt. I cannot communicate without words, but when I am using words I am also using silences. You will have to be aware of both. What I have said to you is less important than the gaps, gaps between two words that I have used. If only words are being understood then it is a communication. And if you can become aware of the gaps also, then it is a communion. But that is altogether up to you.

Begin from somewhere, because one has to begin from somewhere. And every beginning is bound to be a false beginning – but one has to begin from somewhere. And also, through every beginning there is bound to be a false beginning, because in the beginning you cannot know the end – and without knowing the end you cannot know the beginning. The beginning is the past, and you have to begin from somewhere. It is bound to be false but let it be false.

Begin, because through the false, through the groping, is the door. We are in the dark; we have to begin from somewhere. And one who is very wise and who thinks "I will begin only when the right beginning is there," will never begin. He will never grope in the dark because he will say, "When the door is open and I know that this is the door, only then will I take the first step." He will never take the first step, and if the first is not taken, the last can never be reached. And I also say that even a false step is a step; even a false step is a step toward the right step, because it is a step, it is a beginning.

So I also say that even a false beginning, a wrong beginning, is a right beginning because it is a beginning. You begin to grope in the dark and through groping is the door.

## The Mystery of Meditation

That's why I say to be aware of the linguistic process — the process of words — and also seek the awareness of the gaps, the intervals. And there will be moments without your conscious effort, there will be moments and you will become aware of the gap. That is the encounter, the encounter with the divine, the encounter with the existential. Whenever there is encounter, don't escape from it so soon. Be with it. It will be fearful for the first time; it is bound to be.

Whenever the unknown is encountered, fear is created, because to us the unknown means death. We are fearful of death because it is the unknown — the most unknown, or the most *known* unknown. So whenever there is a gap, you will feel death, death coming to you. Then be dead! Just be in it, and die completely in the gap, and you will be resurrected. That's what I mean by resurrection: dying in the gap, in the silence, life is resurrected. You come alive and for the first time, really alive.

So to me, meditation is not a method, but a process; meditation is not a technique, but an understanding. It cannot be taught; it can only be indicated. You cannot be informed about it because really no information is *in*formation. It is from the *out*. Meditation comes from your own inner depths.

So be on a search, be a seeker, and don't be a disciple, because only a seeker is a disciple — but then he is not the disciple of some guru, then he is a disciple of the whole of life. Then, don't go on learning words because a spiritual learning can never be of words. Go on learning gaps — the silences that are there, always surrounding you. They are there even in the crowd, in the market, in the bazaar — they are there. Seek the silences, seek the gaps within and without, and one day you will find that you are in meditation.

Meditation has come to you. It always comes. One has to be in search for it, because only when you are in search are you open to it, vulnerable. You are a host to it, and meditation is a guest. You can invite it and wait for it. It comes. It has always been coming. It comes to a Buddha, it comes to a Jesus, it comes to everybody, anybody who is ready to be open and seeking.

But don't learn it from somewhere; otherwise you will be tricked and the tricks are many. And mind is always searching for easier things – the least resistance. Mind is always for the least resistance and this urge for least resistance becomes the source for exploitation. Then there are gurus and gurudoms, and the whole spiritual search is poisoned.

The most dangerous person is one who exploits someone's spiritual urge. If someone robs you of your wealth it is not so serious, because a thing stolen is not so serious; if someone even kills you it is not so serious, really. But if someone tricks you and kills or even postpones your urge toward meditation, toward the divine, toward the ecstasy, then the sin is great, unforgivable.

But that is being done, so be aware of it. It would be better… Don't ask anybody, "What is meditation? What is meditation? How to meditate?" Ask, "What are the hindrances? What are the obstacles? Why are we not in meditation? Where is growth being stopped? Where have we become crippled?" And seek no guru, because gurus are crippling. They cripple. And anyone who gives you ready-made formulas, ready-made formulae, is not a friend but an enemy.

Grope in the dark. That is the destiny, that is the situation, and nothing can be done. It is so: grope in the dark. And the very groping will become the understanding which

## The Mystery of Meditation

liberates. Jesus has said: "Truth liberates. Truth is freedom." Understanding is freedom because truth is always through understanding. It is not something which you will meet and encounter; it is something you will grow into. Truth is not something you will encounter somewhere in time and space. Truth is something you will grow into.

So be in search of understanding, because understanding is the only growth, and the more understanding you become, the more mature, the nearer truth will be. And in some unknown moment – unexpected, because the mind cannot expect that which is beyond mind; unpredictable, because the mind cannot predict that which is not of the mind – in some unexpected, unpredictable moment when understanding comes to a peak, you are in the abyss. You are no more, and meditation is.

When you are no more, you are in meditation. Both cannot exist simultaneously: either you can exist, or meditation. So meditation is never of you; it is always beyond you. When you are in the abyss, meditation is there. Then the ego is not; then you are not. Then the being is. That's what religions mean by God, the ultimate being. That's what religions mean by the ultimate concern. And meditation is the ultimate concern. It is the essence of all religions, of all seekers and of all searches. It is nowhere to be found ready-made. And one who says it, claims it, then be aware of him.

Go on groping. Don't be afraid of failures. Commit failures, but don't commit the same failure again.

That's all; that's enough. To err is human, to forgive is divine and a person who goes on erring in search of truth is always forgiven. It is a promise from the very depths of existence, but one has to grow toward it.

# 3/ Sex, Love and Prayerfulness: Three Steps to the Divine

*Osho,*
*Please describe to us the spiritual significance of sex energy. How can we sublimate and spiritualize sex? Is it possible to have sex, to make love, as a meditation, as a jumping board toward higher levels of consciousness?*

**There is no such thing as sex energy.** Energy is one and the same. Sex is one outlet for it, one direction for it; it is one of the applications of the energy. Life energy is one, but it can manifest in many directions. Sex is one of them. When life energy becomes biological, it becomes sex energy.

Sex is just an application of the life energy. So there is no question of sublimation. If life energy flows in another direction, there is no sex. But it is not a sublimation; it is a transformation.

Sex is the natural, biological flow of life energy, and the lowest application of it. It is natural

## Sex, Love and Prayerfulness: Three Steps to the Divine

because life cannot exist without it, and the lowest because it is the foundation not the peak. When sex becomes the totality, the whole life is just a waste. It is like laying a foundation and going on laying the foundation, without ever building the house for which the foundation is meant.

Sex is just an opportunity for a higher transformation of life energy. As far as it goes it is all right, but when sex becomes the whole, when it becomes the sole outlet for life energy, then it becomes destructive. It can only be the means, not the end. And means are meaningful only when the ends are achieved. When a man abuses the means, the whole purpose is destroyed. If sex becomes the center of life, as it has become, then means are changed into ends. Sex creates the biological foundation for life to exist, to continue. It is a means; it should not become the end.

The moment sex becomes the end, the spiritual dimension is lost. But if sex becomes meditative, then it is directed toward the spiritual dimension. It becomes a stepping stone, a jumping board. There is no need for sublimation, because energy as such is neither sexual nor spiritual. Energy is always neutral. In itself, it is nameless. The name comes from the door through which it flows. The name is not the name of the energy itself; it is the name of the form that the energy takes. When you say "sexual energy," it means energy that flows through a sexual outlet, through a biological outlet. This same energy is spiritual energy when it flows into the divine.

Energy itself is neutral. When it is expressed biologically, it is sex. When it is expressed emotionally, it may become love, it may become hate, it may become anger. When it is expressed intellectually, it may become scientific, it may become literary. When it moves through the body, it becomes physical.

When it moves through the mind, it becomes mental. The differences are not differences of energy as such, but of the applied manifestations of it.

So it is not right to say "sublimation of sex energy." If the outlet of sex is not used, the energy becomes pure again. Energy is always pure. When it is manifested through the divine door it becomes spiritual, but the form is just a manifestation of the energy.

The word *sublimation* has very bad associations. All theories of sublimation are theories of suppression. Whenever you say "sublimation of sex," you have become antagonistic to it. Your condemnation is there in the very word.

You ask what one can do about sex. Anything done directly to sex is a suppression. There are only indirect methods in which you do not concern yourself with sexual energy at all but, rather, seek to open the door to the divine. When the gate to the divine is open, all the energies that are within you begin to flow toward that door. Sex is absorbed. Whenever a higher bliss is possible, the lower forms of bliss become irrelevant. You are not to suppress them or fight against them. They just wither away. Sex is not sublimated; it is transcended.

Anything done negatively with sex will not transform the energy. On the contrary, it will create a conflict within you that will be destructive. When you fight with an energy, you are fighting with yourself. No one can win the fight. One moment you will feel that you have won, and the next moment you will feel that sex has won. This will go on continuously. Sometimes there will be no sex and you will feel that you have controlled it, and the next moment you will feel the pull of sex again and everything you seem to have gained

## Sex, Love and Prayerfulness: Three Steps to the Divine

will be lost. No one can win a fight against his own energy.

If your energies are needed somewhere else, somewhere more blissful, sex will disappear. It is not that the energy is sublimated; it is not that you have done something to it. Rather, a new way toward greater bliss has opened for you and automatically, spontaneously, the energy begins to flow toward the new door.

If you are holding stones and suddenly diamonds come your way, you will not even notice that you drop the stones. They will drop by themselves, as if you never had them. You won't even remember your renunciation of them, that you have thrown them away. You won't even realize it. It is not that something has been sublimated. A greater source of happiness has been opened, and the lesser sources have dropped away by themselves.

This is so automatic, so spontaneous, that no positive action against sex is needed. Whenever you are doing anything against any energy it is negative. The real, positive action is not even connected with sex but is concerned with meditation. You will not even know that sex has gone. It has simply been absorbed by the new.

*Sublimation* is an ugly word. It carries a tone of antagonism, of conflict, in it. Sex should be taken for what it is. It is just the biological foundation for life to exist. Do not give it any spiritual or anti-spiritual meaning. Simply understand the fact of it.

When you take it as a biological fact, then you are not concerned with it at all. You become concerned with it only when some spiritual meaning is given to it. So do not give any meaning to it; do not create any philosophy around it. Just see the facts. Do not do anything for it or against it. Let it be as it is; accept it as normal. Don't take an abnormal attitude toward it.

Just as you have eyes and hands, so too you have sex. You are not against your eyes or your hands, so do not be against sex. Then the question of what to do about sex becomes irrelevant. To create a dichotomy for or against sex is meaningless. It is a given fact. You have come into existence through sex, and you have a built-in program to give birth through sex again. You are part of a great continuity. Your body is going to die, so it has a built-in program to create another body to replace it.

Death is certain. That is why sex is so obsessive. You will not be here forever, so you will have to be replaced by a newer body, a replica. Sex is so important because the whole nature insists on it; otherwise man could not continue to be. If it were voluntary, there would be no one left on earth. Sex is so obsessive, so compelling, the sex drive is so intense, because the whole of nature is for it. Without it, life cannot exist.

The reason why sex is so important to religious seekers is because it is so non-voluntary, so compelling, so natural. It has become a criterion to know whether the life energy in a particular person has reached the divine. We cannot know directly that someone has encountered the divine – we cannot know directly that someone has diamonds – but we can know directly whether someone has thrown away the stones, because we are acquainted with stones. We can know directly that someone has transcended sex because we are acquainted with sex.

Sex is so compulsive, so non-voluntary, it is so great a force, that it cannot be transcended until someone has

## Sex, Love and Prayerfulness: Three Steps to the Divine

achieved the divine. So *bramacharya* became a criterion to know whether a person has reached the divine. Then sex, as it exists in normal beings, will not exist for him.

This does not mean that by dropping sex one will achieve the divine. The reverse is a fallacy. The person who has found diamonds throws away the stones he was carrying, but the reverse of this is not true. You can throw away the stones, but that doesn't mean you have achieved something beyond it.

Then you will be in between. You will have a suppressed mind, not a transcended one. Sex will go on bubbling inside you and will create an inner hell. This is not going beyond sex. When sex becomes suppressed it becomes ugly, diseased, neurotic. It becomes perverted.

The so-called religious attitude toward sex has created a perverted sexuality, a culture that is completely neurotic sexually. I am not in favor of it. Sex is a biological fact; there is nothing wrong in it. So do not fight it or it will become perverted, and a perverted sex is not a step forward. It is falling below normality; it is a step toward insanity. When the suppression becomes so intense that you cannot prolong it, then it explodes – and in that explosion, you will be lost.

You are *all* human qualities, you are *all* possibilities. The normal fact of sex is healthy, but when it becomes abnormally suppressed it becomes unhealthy. You can move toward the divine from the normal very easily, but to move to the divine from a neurotic mind becomes arduous and, in a way, impossible. First you will have to become healthy, normal. Then, in the end, there is a possibility that sex may be transcended.

Then what is to be done? Know sex! Move into it consciously! This is the secret to open up a new door. If you go into sex unconsciously, then you are just an instrument in the hands of biological evolution, but if you can be conscious in the sex act, the very consciousness becomes a deep meditation.

The sex act is so involuntary and so compulsive that it is difficult to be conscious in it, but it is not impossible. And if you can be conscious in the sex act, then there is no other act in life in which you cannot be conscious, because no act is as deep as sex.

If you can become aware in the sex act, then even in death you will be aware. The depth of the sex act and the depth of death are the same, parallel. You come to the same point. So if you can be aware in the sex act you have achieved a great thing. It is invaluable.

So use sex as an act of meditation. Do not fight it, do not go against it. You cannot fight with nature; you are part and parcel of it. You must have a friendly, sympathetic attitude toward sex. It is the deepest dialogue between you and nature.

In fact, the sex act is not really a dialogue between a man and a woman. It is a dialogue of man with nature, through woman, and of woman with nature, through man. It is a dialogue with nature. For a moment you are in the cosmic flow; you are in the celestial harmony; you are one with the whole. In this way man is fulfilled through woman, and woman through man.

Man is not whole and woman is not whole. They are two fragments of one whole. So whenever they become one in the sexual act, they can be in harmony with the innermost nature of things, with the Tao. This harmony can be a biological birth for a new being. If you are unaware, that is the only possibility. But if you are aware, the act can become a birth for you, a spiritual birth. You will be twice-born through it.

The moment you participate in it consciously, you become

## Sex, Love and Prayerfulness: Three Steps to the Divine

a witness to it. And once you can become a witness in the sex act you will transcend sex, because in witnessing you become free.

Now the compulsion will not be there. You will not be an unconscious participant. Once you have become a witness in the act, you have transcended it. Now you know that you are not the body alone. The witnessing force in you has known something beyond it.

This "beyond" can be known only when you are deeply within. It is not a surface encounter. When you are bargaining in the market, your consciousness cannot go very deep because the act itself is superficial. As far as man is concerned, the sex act is ordinarily the only act through which one can become a witness to the inner depths.

The more you go into meditation through sex, the less effect sex will have. Meditation will grow from it, and out of the growing meditation a new door will open and sex will wither away. It will not be a sublimation. It will be just like dry leaves falling from a tree. The tree never even knows the leaves are falling. In the same way, you will never even know that the mechanical urge for sex is going.

Create meditation out of sex; make sex an object of meditation. Treat it as a temple and you will transcend it and be transformed. Then sex will not be there, but there will not be any suppression, any sublimation. Sex will just become irrelevant, meaningless. You have grown beyond it. It makes no sense to you now.

It is just like a child growing up. Now toys are meaningless. He has not sublimated anything; he has not suppressed anything. He has just grown up; he has become mature. Toys are meaningless now. They are childish and now the child is no longer a child.

In the same way, the more you meditate, the less sex will have an appeal to you. And by and by, spontaneously, without a conscious effort to sublimate sex, energy will have a new source to flow to. The same energy that has flowed through sex will now flow through meditation. And when it flows through meditation, the divine door is being opened.

Another thing. You have used the words *sex* and *love*. Ordinarily we use both words as if they have an inner association. They have not. Love comes only when sex has gone. Before that, love is just a lure, a foreplay, and nothing else. It is just preparing the ground for the sex act. It is nothing but an introduction to sex, a preface. So the more sex there is between two persons, the less love there will be because then the preface is not needed.

If two persons are in love, and if there is no sex between them, there will be much romantic love. But the moment sex comes in, love goes out. Sex is so abrupt. In itself, it is so violent. It needs an introduction; it needs foreplay. Love, as we know it, is just clothing for the naked fact of sex. If you look deeply into what you call love you will find sex standing there, preparing to jump. It is always around the corner. Love is talking; sex is preparing.

This so-called love is associated with sex, but only as a preface. If sex comes, then the love will drop. That's why marriage kills romantic love, and kills it absolutely. The two persons become acquainted with each other and the foreplay, the love, becomes unnecessary.

Real love is not a preface. It is a fragrance. It is not before sex, but after. It is not a prologue but an epilogue. If

## Sex, Love and Prayerfulness: Three Steps to the Divine

you have passed through sex and feel compassion for the other, then love develops. And if you meditate, you will feel compassionate. If you meditate in the sex act, then your sexual partner will not be just an instrument for your physical pleasure. You will feel gratitude to him or her because you have both come to a deep meditation.

When you meditate in sex, a new friendliness will arise between the two of you because, through each other, you have come into communion with nature; through each other, you have had a glimpse into the unknown depths of reality. You will feel grateful and compassionate to each other: compassion for the suffering; compassion for the search; compassion for a fellow being, a fellow traveler.

If sex becomes meditative, only then is there a fragrance that lingers behind: a feeling that is not a foreplay of sex but a maturity, a growth, a meditative realization. So if the sex act becomes meditative, you will feel love. Love is a combination of gratefulness, friendliness and compassion. If these three are there, then you are in love.

If this love develops, it will transcend sex. Love develops through sex, but goes beyond it. Just like a flower it comes through the roots, but goes beyond. And it will not come back; there is no reversal. So if love develops, no sex will be there. In fact, that is one of the ways of knowing that love has developed. Sex is like the shell of an egg, a shell through which love has to emerge. The moment it emerges, the shell will no longer be there. It will be broken, discarded.

Sex can reach love only when meditation is there, otherwise not. If meditation is not there, the same sex will be repeated and you will become bored. Sex will become increasingly dull, and you will not feel grateful to the other.

Rather, you will feel cheated; you will feel inimical to him. He dominates you. He dominates through sex, because it has become a need for you. You have become a slave because you cannot live without sex. You can never feel friendly toward someone to whom you have become a slave.

Both will feel the same: that the other is the master. The domination will be denied and fought, but sex will still be repeated. It will become a daily routine. You fight with your sex partner, and then make things right again. Then again you fight; then again you make up. Love is just an adjustment at the most. You cannot feel friendly; there is no compassion. Instead there will be cruelty and violence; you will feel cheated. You have become a slave, sex will not be able to develop into love. It will remain just sex.

Go through sex! Do not be afraid of it, because fear leads nowhere. If one has to be afraid of anything, it is only of fear itself. Do not fear sex and do not fight it because that too is a sort of fear. "Fight or flight" – fight or escape – these are two paths of fear. So do not escape sex; do not fight it. Accept it, take it for granted. Go deep in it, know it totally, understand it, meditate in it – and you will transcend it. The minute you meditate in the sex act, a new door is opened. You come upon a new dimension, a very unknown, unheard-of one, and greater bliss flows through.

You will encounter something so blissful that sex will become irrelevant and it will subside by itself. Now your energy will no longer flow in that direction. Energy always flows toward bliss. Because bliss appears in sex, energy flows toward it, but if you seek more bliss – a bliss that transcends sex, that goes beyond sex, a bliss that is more fulfilling, deeper, greater – then, by itself, energy will stop flowing toward sex.

## Sex, Love and Prayerfulness: Three Steps to the Divine

When sex becomes a meditation it flowers into love, and this flowering is a movement toward the divine. That is why love is divine. Sex is physical; love is spiritual. And if the flower of love is there, prayerfulness will come; it will follow. Now you are not far from the divine. You are near home.

Now, begin to meditate on love. This is the second step. When the moment of communion is there, when the moment of love is there, begin to meditate. Go deep in it; be aware of it. Now bodies are not meeting. In sex, bodies were meeting; in love, souls are meeting. It is still a meeting, a meeting between two persons.

Now, see love as you have seen sex. See the communion, the inner meeting, the inner intercourse. Then you will transcend even love, and you will come to prayerfulness. This prayerfulness is the door. It is still a meeting, but not a meeting between two persons. It is a communion between you and the whole. Now the other, as a person, is dropped. It is the impersonal other – the whole existence – and you.

But prayerfulness is still a meeting, so ultimately it also has to be transcended. In prayerfulness, the devotee and the divine are different; the *bhakta* and the *bhagwan* are different. It is still a meeting. That is why Meera, or Theresa, could use sexual terms for their prayerful experiences.

One must meditate in prayerful moments. Again, be a witness to it. See the communion between you and the whole. This requires the subtlest awareness possible. If you can be aware of the meeting between you and the whole, then you transcend both yourself and the whole. Then you *are* the whole. And in this whole, there is no duality; there is only oneness.

This oneness is sought through sex, through love, through

prayerfulness. This oneness is what is longed for. Even in sex, the longing is for the oneness. Bliss comes because, for a single moment, you have become one. Sex deepens into love, love deepens into prayerfulness, and prayerfulness deepens into a total transcendence, a total oneness.

This deepening is always through meditation. The method is always the same. Levels differ, dimensions differ, steps differ, but the method is the same. Dig into sex and you will find love. Go deep into love and you will come to prayerfulness. Dig into prayerfulness and you will explode into oneness. This oneness is the total, this oneness is the bliss, this oneness is the ecstasy.

So it is essential not to take a fighting attitude. In every fact, the divine is present. It may be garbed, it may be clothed, but you must strip it, unclothe it. You will find still more subtle garbs. Again, undress it. Unless you encounter the oneness in its total nakedness, you will not find satisfaction, you will not feel fulfilled.

The moment you come to the ungarbed one, the unclothed one, you become one with it, because when you know the naked, it is no one but you. In fact, everyone is searching for himself through others. One has to find one's own home by knocking on others' doors.

The moment reality is disrobed you are one with it, because the difference is only of garbs. Clothes are the barrier, so you cannot disrobe reality unless you disrobe yourself. That is why meditation is a double weapon: it disrobes reality and it disrobes you as well. The reality becomes naked, and you become naked. And in a moment of total nakedness, total emptiness, you become one.

I am not against sex. That doesn't mean I am for sex. It

## Sex, Love and Prayerfulness: Three Steps to the Divine

means that I am for going deep in it and uncovering the beyond. The beyond is always there, but ordinary sex is hit-and-run sex, so no one goes deep. If you can go deep, you will feel grateful to the divine that through sex a door is opened. But if sex is just hit-and-run, you will never know that you were close to something greater.

We are so cunning that we have created a false love, that does not come after sex but before it. It is a cultivated, artificial thing. That's why we feel that love is lost when sex is fulfilled. Love was just the preface, and now the preface is no longer needed. But real love is always beyond sex; it is hiding behind sex. Go deep in it, meditate in it religiously, and you will flower into a loving state of mind.

I am not against sex and I am not for love. You still have to transcend it. Meditate on it; transcend it. By meditation I mean you have to pass through it fully alert, aware. You must not pass through it blindly, unconsciously. Great bliss is there, but you can pass by blindly and miss it. This blindness has to be transformed; you must become open-eyed. With open eyes, sex can take you on the path of oneness.

The drop can become the ocean. That is the longing within every drop's heart. In every act, in every desire, you will find the same longing. Uncover it, follow it. It is a great adventure! As we live our lives today, we are unconscious. But this much can be done; it is arduous, but it is not impossible. It has been possible for a Jesus, for a Buddha, for a Mahavira, and it is possible for everyone else.

When you go into sex with this intensity, with this alertness, with this sensitivity, you will transcend it. There will not be any sublimation at all. When you transcend, there will be no sex, not even sublimated sex. There will be love, prayerfulness, and oneness.

These are the three stages of love: physical love, psychic love and spiritual love. And when these three are transcended, there is the divine. When Jesus said, "God is love," this was the closest definition possible, because the last thing we know on the path toward godliness is love. Beyond that is the unknown, and the unknown cannot be defined. We can only indicate the divine through our last realization: love. Beyond that point of love, there is no experience because there is no experiencer. The drop has become the ocean.

Go step by step, but with a friendly attitude, with no tension, no struggle. Just go with alertness. Alertness is the only light in the dark night of life. With this light, go into it. Seek and search every corner. Everywhere is the divine, so do not be against anything.

But do not remain with anything either. Go beyond, because still greater bliss awaits you. The journey must continue. If you are near sex, use sex. If you are near love, use love. Do not think in terms of suppression or sublimation; do not think in terms of fighting. The divine may be hiding behind anything, so do not fight. Do not escape from anything. In fact, it is behind everything, so wherever you are, take the closest door and you will progress. Do not become stagnant anywhere and you will reach, because life is everywhere.

Jesus said, "Under every stone is the Lord," but you see only the stones. You will have to pass through this stony state of mind. When you see sex as an enemy, it becomes a stone. Then it becomes non-transparent; you cannot see beyond it. Use it, meditate on it, and the stone will become just like glass. You will see behind it, and you will forget the glass.

## Sex, Love and Prayerfulness: Three Steps to the Divine

What is behind the glass will be remembered.

Anything that becomes transparent will disappear. So do not make sex a stone, make it transparent. And it becomes transparent through meditation.

# 4 / Kundalini Yoga: Returning to the Roots

*Osho,*
*What is kundalini? What is kundalini yoga and how can kundalini yoga help the West? And also why is your method for awakening kundalini chaotic rather than like the traditional, controlled methods?*

**Existence is energy,** the movement of energy in so many shapes and so many forms. Kundalini is one of them, as far as human existence is concerned. Kundalini is the focused energy of the human body and the human psyche.

Energy can exist unmanifest or manifest. It can remain in the seed, or it can come up in the manifested form. Every energy is either in the seed or in the manifested form. Kundalini means your total potential, your total possibility. But it isn't a seed; it is the potential. It can become actual but it is not actual. The ways of working on kundalini are the ways of making your potential actual.

So first, kundalini is not something unique. It is human energy as such, but ordinarily it is not functioning, or only a part is functioning, a very minute part is functioning. And that part too is not functioning harmoniously; it is in conflict. That's the misery, that's the anguish. If your energy can function harmoniously then you feel blissful; if it works in conflict – in itself, antagonistic – then you feel miserable. All misery is your energy in conflict, and all happiness – all bliss – is your energy in harmony.

Why is the potential, the whole potential, not actual? Firstly, it is not needed as far as day-to-day life is concerned. The whole potential is not needed, it is not challenged, it is not required. Only that part becomes functioning which is required, challenged and tapped. Day-to-day life is not a challenge to it, so only a very minute part becomes manifest. This part is also not harmonious. It is doubly in conflict – one conflict is within, within this very part. It is not integrated because the day-to-day life is not integrated.

Requirements are in conflict. Needs are in conflict. Your society requires something, your instincts require something else, quite contradictory. In the morning something is required and in the afternoon you go quite contrary to it. You have to go... The day-to-day needs are in conflict. The social requirement and the natural requirement are in conflict. The society and its requirements, the morality, the religion, and their requirements – they have never been in search of a harmonious whole. They are fragmentary. Everything is meaningful in itself, but not in the organic unity of the human being.

Your wife requires something from you; your mother

requires something quite contrary. Then your day-to-day life becomes a conflicting demand on you. The part, the minute part, that becomes manifest in you – the energy, the potential that becomes actual – is fragmentary, in conflict within itself.

This is one level of conflict and contradictions. Another is, the part which becomes manifest will always be in conflict with the part which has not yet become manifest. The actual will always be in conflict with the potential, because the potential will push itself to be manifested, and the actual will suppress it.

To use psychological terms, the unconscious will always be in conflict with the conscious. The conscious will try to dominate it, because with the potential and its urge to manifest, the conscious is always in danger – because the conscious is under control and the potential is not, the unconscious is not. With the conscious you can manage, but with the explosion of the unconscious you will be in an insecurity. You will not be able to manage it. That's the fear, the fear with the conscious – the mind part is always in fear of the major portion which is unconscious and has been pushed away. So there is another conflict – greater, vital and more deep a conflict – between the conscious and the unconscious; the energy which has become manifest and the energy which wants to be manifested.

These two conflicts, these two types of conflicts, are why you are not in harmony. And if you are not in harmony then your energies will become enemies to you. Energy needs movement, and movement is always from the unmanifest toward the manifest, from the seed toward the tree. It is always from the dark toward the light.

Energy needs movement and movement is possible only

## Kundalini Yoga: Returning to the Roots

if there is no suppression. Otherwise the movement, the harmony, is destroyed and your energies turn into enemies against yourself. Then you become a house divided in itself, then you are not organic, then you become a crowd. Then you are not one, then you become many.

This is the situation as human beings exist. It should not be, because this is the ugliness and this is the misery. All bliss that is possible and all beatitude that is possible can come only when your life energy is in movement – and in easy movement, in relaxed movement, unsuppressed, uninhibited; integral and not fragmentary; not in conflict within itself, but one and organic, complementary, cooperative. If this happens that is what is meant by kundalini.

If your energies come to this harmonious, organic unity, the technical term in yoga for it is kundalini. It is just a technical term: all your energies in unity, in movement, in harmony, without any conflict; cooperative, complementary and organic. Then…then there is a transformation, unique and unknown.

When energies are in conflict, you are just relieving them. You are relaxed when your conflicting energies are released. Whenever you can brush them off, wash them off, you are released. You feel at ease. Only then are your energies thrown off. And whenever your energies are thrown off, your life, your vitality, your élan vital is downward, or outward – and both are the same.

The downward movement is the outward movement, and the upward movement is the inward movement. The more your energies go up, the more they go in. The more your energies go down, the more they go out. You can wash off your energies only if you throw them out. This is just like throwing off your own life, throwing yourself into bits and fragments, in installments. This is suicidal.

But we are all suicidal unless our life energies becomes one and harmonious, and the flow becomes inward. This is the same as upward, because inwardness is upwardness: the more you go in, the more you go up. These are not two dimensions: one dimension – up and in, and another direction – down and out. Unless energies are organic you are just wasting them. But through waste, through wastage, you feel relieved.

Of course, the relief is bound to be momentary because you are a constant source of energies. They will be coming again. You are a flow; you are a flow of vital forces. They will come up again. They will come up in you again and you will have to get rid of them again.

So whatsoever is known as pleasure ordinarily is just the pleasure of throwing off conflicting energies. Pleasure means relief – you are relieved of a burden. So pleasure is always negative, it is never positive. Bliss is positive. It comes only when your energies are fulfilled.

When your energies are not thrown out but have a flowering inward, when you become one with your energies and are not in conflict with them, then there is a movement inward. That movement is endless because there is no end to inwardness. It goes on, deeper and deeper, and the deeper it goes, the more blissful it becomes, the more ecstatic.

So energies can have two possibilities. One is just of relief, just throwing energies which have become burdensome to you into fragments – which you could not utilize, with which you could not be creative, with which you could not be one and organic, so you have to throw them. This is "anti-kundalini," a state of mind.

## Kundalini Yoga: Returning to the Roots

The ordinary state of human beings is anti-kundalini. It is just like forces going from the center toward the periphery – the movement is periphery-oriented. Kundalini means just the contrary. It is center-oriented – forces coming from the periphery to the center.

The center is not the end. The center is as infinite as the periphery. If you throw your energies outward they will go on and on, outward and outward, and there is no end to the space. If energies are directed inward then, too, there is no end. But the movement inward – the center-oriented movement – is blissful. The outward movement is both, it is both. Momentarily it gives happiness and permanently, misery. It will be a permanent misery. Only in gaps…and that too not actually, but only when you hope, you expect, is the gap. The actual result is always misery.

In expectation, in hoping, in waiting, in desiring, in dreaming, is the moment of happiness. And when you are actually relieved of your burden, the state of the mind is totally negative. There is no happiness as such, but only absence of misery for a moment. That absence is taken as happiness.

Other energies will be coming to the periphery because the moment is always there. You are toward the periphery; other energies will be coming there. And you are creating your own enemy; you are constantly creating new energies. That's what is meant by "life": the ability to go on creating life force. The moment the capacity is gone, you are dead. So you are a constant dilemma, a constant creative force. But this is the paradox: you go on creating energy and you don't know what to do with it. When it is created you throw it off; when it is not created you feel miserable, you feel ill.

The moment the life force is not being created, you feel

ill. But when it is created, you again feel ill. The first illness is that of weakness, and the second illness is that of…that of an energy which has become a burden to you. You were not able to harmonize it, to make it creative, to make it blissful. You have created it and now you don't know what to do with it, so you throw it off, just wash it off. And you are creating this! This is absurd, but this absurdity is ordinarily what we mean by human existence: constantly creating energy and it constantly becoming burdensome – and then you have to be relieved of it.

That's why sex has become so important, so significant, because that is one of the greatest instruments to wash off energy, one of the greatest outlets. If a society becomes affluent, you have more sources through which energy can be created. Then you become more sexual because then you have to release more; this constant creating and throwing!

So if one is intelligent enough, sensitive enough, then one will feel the boredom, the absurdity of it, the whole meaninglessness of it. Then one will feel the purposelessness of life. Are you just an instrument for creating energy and throwing it off? Then what is the meaning? Then what is the need to exist at all? – just to be an instrument in which energy is created, a mechanical device in which energy is created and thrown off? So the more sensitive a person is, the more he will feel it – the meaninglessness of the totality of life as it is, as it is lived, as we know it.

Kundalini means to change this absurd situation into a meaningful one. The science of kundalini is one of the most subtle of sciences, because as far as physical sciences are concerned, they too are concerned with energy as such, but with material energy, not psychic energy. Yoga is concerned with psychic energy as such. It is a science of the metaphysical, of that which is transcendental to physics – the psychic energy.

This psychic energy can be creative or can be destructive. If it is not used it becomes destructive. If it is used it becomes creative. It can be used and it can be made creative. The way to make it creative is first to understand that you should not be partially realized. One part realized and the remaining, major, portion of your potential unrealized is not a situation which can be creative.

The whole must be realized. Your whole potential must be actualized. So there are methods to realize the remaining potential, to make it actual, to make it awake. It is sleeping just like a snake sleeping. That's why it has been named "kundalini": serpent power, a serpent sleeping.

If you have seen a serpent sleeping, it is just as if dead; there is no movement at all, and it is encircled. You cannot conceive that a serpent can stand, but a serpent *can* stand. It can stand on its tail, upright, straight; a serpent stands just as an energy. That's why it has been used symbolically. Serpent power is used symbolically. Your life energy is encircled and asleep, but it can stand. And if it can be awake, with full potential actualized, you will be transformed.

Life and death are only two states of energy. Life means energy functioning; death means non-functioning. Life means energy awake; death means energy gone again into sleep. So according to kundalini yoga, ordinarily you are partially alive. The part of your energies which has become actualized is your life. And a very minute part is alive. The remaining is just as if it is not.

So it can be tapped and there are so many methods through

which kundalini yoga tries to make the potential actual. For example, *pranayama*. It is one of the methods to hammer the asleep energy. Through breath, hammering is possible, because breathing is the bridge between your élan vital – your *prana*, your original source of vitality – and your actual existence. Between the potential and the actual, breath is the bridge.

The moment you change your breathing system, your total energy system is changed. When you are asleep your breathing changes. When you are awake your breathing changes. When you are in anger your breathing is different, when you are in love your breathing is different, when you are in a sexual passion then your breathing is quite different, because in every state of mind you require different quantities of life force, so your breathing changes.

When you are in anger you require more energy toward the periphery. From the center toward the periphery you require more energy. You are in danger, or you are to attack or you are to defend – more energy is needed on the boundaries so the center will rush with the energy.

That's why in anger you begin to tremble. Your eyes go red. Your blood pressure will rise, and your breathing will be as…as to be helpful to the energy to move toward the periphery. When you are in sexual passion, you need energy, more energy toward the periphery. That's why after a sexual act you feel exhausted, because you have thrown a great quantity of energy from your body – an unusual quantity.

After anger you will also feel exhausted. But after a loving moment you will never feel exhausted; you will feel refreshed. After being prayerful, you will feel refreshed. Why? Why has the contrary happened? When you are in a loving moment, no energy is needed on the periphery because there is no question of attack, defense. There is no insecurity, there is no danger. You are at ease, relaxed, so the energy flows inward. When energy flows inward you feel refreshed.

After a deep sleep you feel refreshed, because energy flows inward. Whenever energy flows inward you feel...you feel vitalized, you feel fulfilled. You feel a well-being.

And another thing to be noted: whenever energy is going inward, your breath will have a quite different quality. It will be relaxed, settled, rhythmic, harmonious. And there will be moments when you will not feel it at all. There will be moments when you will feel as if it has stopped. It becomes so subtle, because energy is not needed so the bridge is dropped. The flow is not needed so the instrument is dropped.

In *samadhi*, in ecstasy, one feels a complete stoppage. The in breath remains in, the out breath remains out – and there is a gap. Everything has stopped. No outward flow is needed, so breath is unnecessary.

Through *pranyam* this energy which is as yet potential is made systematically actual. Through asanas, also, kundalini potential can be tapped because your body postures are connected. Your body is connected from everywhere with the source of energy. You cannot go to sleep standing – you'll feel it difficult – but if you are exhausted and have not been asleep for a long time, then you can even go to sleep standing. But in *siksasan*, standing upside down, you cannot go to sleep. The posture is antagonistic to sleep because the blood is flowing toward the mind. That's why one uses pillows, and the more a person becomes civilized and educated, the more pillows will be needed.

Uncivilized aboriginals will not need pillows – why? Because if blood is flowing toward your mind, and your mind has a mechanical habit to go on functioning, and if blood is supplied, it will go on functioning. You will not be able to sleep. So you change the posture: a pillow is just changing your posture. Your head is now not parallel to your body and blood circulation will be less and the functioning will drop.

Every posture has a corresponding effect on the original energy source, so yoga uses asanas. For example, *siddhasan*, the posture that Buddha uses, *padmasana*. This posture is one of the postures in which the least energy is needed, the least energy is needed to exist. In any other posture of the body, more energy is needed. Buddha's posture is the least energy-using posture. If you are standing upright, you use more energy. If you are sitting and not upright, you use more energy because the gravitational pull is there. But sitting upright is so balanced; you become one with the earth. You have no pull. And if your hands and feet are in such a position that a circuit is created, the life energy, life electricity, will flow in a circuit.

So Buddha's posture is a round posture. Energy becomes circular; it is not thrown off, because energy is always washed out through the fingers of the hands or toes of the feet. Through round shapes the energy cannot flow out. Round shapes cannot become outlets. That's why women are more resistant to illness, more resistant to tiredness, and anyway, more powerful than men. They resist death more and one of the reasons is their round shape, roundness of the body. Less energy flows outward.

As far as the sexual act is concerned women will not be so exhausted after the act because of the shape of their sexual organ. It is round and absorbing. Men will be more exhausted because of the shape of their sexual organ. More energy is thrown out – not only biological energy, but psychic energy also.

So if you see Buddha's posture then you will be amazed. All the outlets are connected. Both feet are crossed, both hands are crossed, and hands touch the feet and feet touch the sexual center, the sex center. All the energy outlets are conjoined in Buddha's posture – no energy can go out and the posture is erect so there is no gravitational pull.

And in that posture one can forget the body completely. You can forget the body completely only when life is not flowing outward; otherwise you cannot forget it. So one becomes encircling energy and one can forget life; one can forget the body completely. Eyes are closed or half closed, because eyes are also a great outlet for psychic energy. They're closed or half closed. In both situations the result is the same, and the movements of the eyeball are stopped. If the eyeballs are moving then energy is being thrown out.

Even in dreaming you throw much energy out through eye movements. The only way of knowing whether a person is dreaming or not is through his eyeballs, to know outwardly whether he is dreaming or not. If you put your fingers on his eyes and if they are moving, then he is dreaming. Awaken him and you will find that he was dreaming. If the eyeballs are not moving then he is not dreaming. If the eyeballs are not moving then he is in deep sleep, *sushupti*. Then all energies are going inward; nothing is going outward. Then the whole process is inward.

Asanas, *pranyam* – and there are so many other methods through which energies can be made to flow inward. When they flow inward they become one, because in the center they cannot be many. Only on the periphery can they be many. In the center they are bound to be one and organic. On the periphery they will be many. The more energy goes inward, the more harmonious. Conflicts are dropped and in the center there is no conflict. There is an organic unity of the whole. That's why bliss is felt.

Another thing. These are bodily helps, and they are significant and they are important – but they are only physical helps. If your mind is in conflict then they will not be of much help. Your body and mind are not two things actually. Your body and mind are two poles of one thing. You are not body *and* mind; you are body-mind. You are psycho-somatic or somato-psychic.

Our language is faulty. We use the body as something different and the mind as something different, and sometimes we define body as "not mind," and mind as "not body." That error has crept into all languages of the world because of the dualistic philosophy that has prevailed all over the world. Body and mind are two poles of one energy. Body is gross, mind is subtle, but the energy is the same.

So one has to work from both of the polarities. From the body you have hatha yoga: asanas, *pranyam*, etcetera. They help to make the potential actual. And from the mind you have to use raja yoga and other yogas which are basically concerned with your mental attitudes.

For example, if you can control your breath when there is anger, anger will die. If you can go on breathing rhythmically, anger cannot overpower you. If you go on breathing rhythmically, sexual passion cannot overpower you. It will go, but it will be suppressed, because this is only a physical part. It will not become manifest. No one will know it, not even you yourself will be able to know it. It can be so suppressed through breathing; through rhythmic breathing you can suppress anger so much that you yourself will not be aware of it. But it will be there, because you have tackled it only through one part of your being, body. The other part remains untouched.

So one has to work both ways. The body should be trained through yogic methodology, and the mind through awareness. And you will need more awareness if you practice yoga, because things will become more subtle.

If you are angry, ordinarily you can become aware of it: that is not very arduous, the anger is so gross. But if you practice *pranyam*, then you will need more awareness, more acute sensitivity to be aware of anger, because now anger will become more subtle, because one part, body, which can make it gross, is not cooperating with it, so it will be just a mental way, with no physical expression at all. It will be very subtle.

So those persons who practice awareness, if they also simultaneously practice yogic methodology, then they will know that awareness has deeper realms. Otherwise they will be only aware of the gross. And if you can change the gross and cannot change the subtle, you will be in a dilemma, in a great dilemma, because now the conflict will assert itself in a new way. The conflict will assert itself between your mind and your body.

So yoga is helpful, but is not the be all and end all, it is only a part. Another part is mental attitude, which Buddha has called "mindfulness." Practice yoga so that the body is not inimical to you, the body is not contradictory to you, the body is rhythmic and with you, and the body is cooperating with the inward movement. Then practice mindfulness. Both should be done simultaneously.

Be mindful of breathing. In yoga, you are to change the breathing process. In mindfulness, you have to be aware of breathing itself, as it is – just awareness of the breathing. If you can become aware of breathing, then you can become aware of your thought processes; otherwise not.

Those who try to be directly aware of thought processes will not be able to do that. It will be very arduous because breathing is the door to the mind. You will be surprised, if you can stop your breath for a single moment, you will see simultaneously your thoughts have stopped. Here, breathing stops; there, the thought process is broken. Stop the breath and thought is stopped; continue the thought process vigorously and you will see that the breathing is chaotic – simultaneously. Breathing will reflect your thought processes.

First become mindful of the breathing. Buddha says "*anapanasati yog*": the yoga of awareness of the incoming and outgoing breath. And he says, "Begin from here," and that is a right beginning. One should begin from breathing and never from the thought process itself, because one should begin from the gross to the subtle – from the body first; second, from awareness of the breath. When you become aware of the breath and when you can feel subtle movements of the breath, only then will you be able to feel the subtle nuances of thought.

Awareness of thought processes will change the quality of the mind; asanas, *pranyam*, will change the quality of the body. And they both synchronize, and a moment comes when your body and mind are one, without conflict – without any conflict at all – when they are one, when there is a synthetic movement. They are synthesized, they synchronize. Then, in that moment, you are neither body nor mind. For the first time, in this synthetic moment, you know yourself as the self. You transcend.

You can only transcend when there is no conflict; otherwise there is no transcendence. This moment, this harmonious moment of body and mind – when they are both one, with no conflict, and energy is coming inward or upward – you transcend both. Then you are neither. Now you are something which is not a "thing" at all. You are nothing in a sense, "no thing" in a sense. Now you are simply consciousness – not conscious about something, but only consciousness; not aware of something, but only awareness.

This realization of awareness without being aware of anything, this realization of consciousness without being conscious of anything, is the moment of explosion. Your potential becomes actual. You explode into a new realm – the ultimate. This ultimate is the concern of all the religions.

And there are so many ways. One may talk of kundalini or not; that is immaterial. *Kundalini* is only a word. You can use another word. You can call it anything, it makes no difference. But that which is signified by *kundalini* is bound to be there in some way or other – a synthetic inward flow.

This inward flow is the only revolution, or the only freedom. Otherwise you will go on creating more hells, because the more you go outward, the more far off you are from yourself. And the more far off you are, the more ill, the more diseased – because the original source of all life is cut off in so many ways from you. You become an outsider to yourself and you don't know how to come back home. This coming back is the science of yoga. And kundalini yoga is the subtlest science – the supreme – as far as human transformation is concerned.

And you have also asked: "Traditional methods are systematic and your method is chaotic – why is it so?" Traditional methods are systematic because for the person, for the persons and for the people for whom they were developed, they were different.

Modern man is a very new phenomenon, and no traditional method can be used exactly as it exists, because modern man has never existed before. Modern man is a new phenomenon. So in a way, all traditional methods have become irrelevant. Their spirit is not irrelevant, but their form has become irrelevant because this man is new.

For example, the body has changed so much. It is not natural now, as it always was. The human body today is a very unnatural thing. When Patanjali developed his yoga, the body was a natural phenomena. Now it is not a natural phenomena. It is absolutely different; it is so drugged that no traditional method can be helpful.

Medicine was not allowed to be given to hatha yogis, absolutely not allowed, because chemical changes would make methods not only difficult, but harmful – so medicine was not allowed, or special medicines were developed. The whole atmosphere is artificial now: the air is artificial, the water is artificial, the society's living conditions are artificial. Nothing is natural. You are born in this artificiality; you develop in it, so traditional methods will prove harmful. They cannot be used as they are. They will have to be changed according to the modern, the modern situation.

Another thing. The quality of the mind has changed. Basically in Patanjali's days, in olden days, the center of the

## Kundalini Yoga: Returning to the Roots

human personality was not the brain; it was the heart. And before that, it was not even the heart. It was still lower, near the navel. In the pre-Patanjali days, before Patanjali, it was the navel – the center of human personality. So hatha yoga developed methods which were useful, meaningful, to the person whose center of personality was the navel. Then the center became the heart. When the center became the heart, then only bhakti yoga could be applied, otherwise not. So bhakti yoga developed in the Middle Ages – never before – because the center changed. And a method has to change according to the people to whom it is applied.

Now, even bhakti yoga is not relevant. The main center has again gone still further from the navel. Now, it is the brain. That's why teachings like Krishnamurti appeal, because the center is the brain. Otherwise, they will have no appeal; they will have no appeal at all. So no method is needed, no technique is needed. Only understanding is needed. But when we say "understanding" it becomes intellectual, and nothing else. It is just verbal understanding. It makes no change, it transforms nothing. It again becomes accumulation of knowledge. It again becomes memory.

So when I use chaotic methods and not systematic ones to push this center from the brain, chaotic methods are very helpful. Through any systematic method the center cannot be pushed below the brain, because systematization is work of the brain. You systematize everything *through* the brain. So if you use systematic methods the brain will be more strengthened. It will take energy in itself.

So I use chaotic methods because through chaotic methods the brain is nullified. It has nothing to do. There is no system to be made and no mathematical formula to be applied. It is so chaotic that the center from the brain is automatically pushed to the heart, and that is a great step – to push the center from the brain to the heart. So if you do my method vigorously, unsystematically, chaotically, your center is pushed lower. You come to the heart.

When you come to the heart then I apply catharsis because your heart is so suppressed – because of your brain: the brain has taken up so much territory within you, so much domination of you, it has absorbed the whole. There is no space for the heart, so longings of the heart have been suppressed. You have never laughed heartily, never cried heartily, never done anything heartily. The brain always comes in to systematize, to make things mathematical. That brain calculates and concludes and comes in. The heart is suppressed.

So first chaotic methods are used to push the center – the center of consciousness – from the brain toward the heart. Then catharsis is needed to unburden the heart, to throw off the suppressions, to make it light. If the heart becomes light and unburdened, then the center of consciousness is pushed still lower. It comes to the navel, and only when it comes to the navel I will ask you to inquire, "Who am I?" Otherwise it is meaningless.

Raman Maharshi's method could not be very successful because he used to ask directly, "Who am I?" Then the brain asks, "Who am I?" The intellect asks, "Who am I?" An intellect is very cunning; it asks and supplies the answer. It asks "Who am I?" then there is an answer accumulating in the memory: "I am the soul, I am the brahman..." The brain supplies the answer. It does both. It plays the game from both the sides – and it is absurd, it cannot be a help.

Ramana could achieve through this method because his

## Kundalini Yoga: Returning to the Roots

center of consciousness was at the navel and never the brain. He was not a man of the brain. In a way he was one of the oldest beings – one of the oldest. He was not of this century. He was not a contemporary to us. His center was the navel, but he…if he says to others ask "Who am I?" it becomes meaningless, because the center is different. They will ask through the brain, and they will reply with an answer through the brain.

Only when your consciousness is at the navel, and you ask, "Who am I?" will the brain never be able to supply the answer. It cannot cross the heart. It cannot come to the navel. There is no way to it. So if the consciousness is at the navel and you ask "Who am I?" then there is a question and no answer. Then the question penetrates deep, and deeper and deeper, and a moment comes when the question itself drops. It is no more. When the question is no more, is the answer. They are never simultaneous. If they are simultaneous – this is the question and this is the answer – then it is brain work. If the question is dead, no more, and the answer comes, then it is navel work.

Then it is quite a different thing. It has come from the source – the source of vitality – and the navel *is* the source of vitality. It is the source, it is the seed source from which everything comes: the body, the mind, all else.

So this chaotic method, I use very meaningfully, very consideredly. Now systematic methodology will not help because the brain will turn it into its own instrument. Now only chanting *bhajans* will not help, because the heart is so much burdened that it cannot flower into a real chanting; it cannot flower. Chanting can only be an escape for it; prayerfulness can only be an escape. It cannot flower into a prayerfulness – the heart cannot flower into a prayerfulness because it is so burdened. It has been so suppressed that authentic prayerfulness has become impossible. I have not seen a single person who can go deep in authentic prayerfulness, because love itself has become impossible.

Consciousness must be pushed down to the source, to the roots. Only then is there the possibility of transformation. So I use a chaotic method to push consciousness from the brain. And whenever you are in chaos the brain stops working, it cannot work.

Whenever you are in chaos, the brain stops. You are driving a car and suddenly someone comes in front of you. You push the brake so suddenly that it is not a work of the brain. It cannot be because the brain takes time: it thinks: what to do, what not to do. So whenever there is a possibility of an accident and you push the brake, you will feel the sensation near your navel, never near your brain. You will feel that your stomach is upset, because your total consciousness is being pushed because of the chaotic accident. If it could be calculated before and predicted then there would be no need, then there would be no need. Mind would do, brain would do. Whenever you are in an accident, unknown, something unknown comes to you, you will see that consciousness comes to the navel.

If you ask a Zen monk, "From where do you think?" he will put his hands to his stomach. When Westerners came in contact with Japanese monks for the first time, they could not understand: "What nonsense! How can you think from the stomach? No one thinks from the stomach." But the Zen reply is meaningful. Consciousness can use any center of the body, and the most primary and the most near to the original source is the navel, and the most far off is the brain. So if life energy goes outward, then ultimately the center of consciousness will become the brain. If life energy goes inward, then ultimately the navel will become the center.

That's why I use this chaotic method, with a cathartic technique – to push the consciousness to its roots – because only from the roots is transformation possible. Otherwise you will only verbalize and go on verbalizing, and there will be no transformation and no change. Even if you know the right things you will not be transformed, because it is not enough to know right things. One has to go to the roots, and one has to change and transform the roots. Otherwise you will not change.

And sometimes a person is in even more difficulty when he knows the right things and cannot do anything. A new impatience, a new tension arises – he becomes doubly tense. He understands and he cannot do. Understanding can only be meaningful when you understand from the navel. Otherwise it is never meaningful. If you understand from the brain, then it is not transforming.

The ultimate, the original, the inner, cannot be known from brain work, because you are in contact with the ultimate from your roots, from where you have come. Your whole problem is having moved away from the navel. You have come from the navel and you will die through it; you have come from that gate and you will pass through that gate. One has to come to that gate, and when you come to the roots there is no difficulty to change. The change is simple, but coming to the roots is difficult and arduous.

Kundalini is concerned with life energy and its inward flow, and with techniques of body and mind to come to a point – a synthetic moment – in which transcendence becomes possible. Then the body is different, the mind is different, the attitude is different, the living is different.

It is just as if something is useful in a bullock cart, but now the bullock cart is no more. You are driving a car, but the bullock cart – its techniques, its instruments – is still with you. The bullock cart has gone but a continuity is there. You cannot use anything from the bullock cart in your car. It doesn't mean that it was not useful in the bullock cart: it was used and it was helpful – it was not wrong. But it is irrelevant in a car.

So one difficulty is: traditional methods are there, they have an appeal because they are so old and ancient – so much tradition with them, so many people have achieved through them. That gives them credit. You can deny traditional methods, but you cannot deny Buddha buddhahood. You cannot deny Patanjali his freedom, you cannot deny Krishna his knowledge. Traditional methods have become irrelevant to us, but they were not irrelevant to Buddha or to Mahavira or to Krishna. They were meaningful, they were used, they were helpful. Now Buddha cannot be denied his buddhahood, but the method is meaningless now. The method has appeal because Buddha cannot be denied – "A Buddha achieved through it, why can't we?" We could have, in a very different situation – altogether different.

The whole mind-sphere, the whole thought-sphere, has changed. So the traditionalist, the conformist will say, "Buddha could achieve through this method or that method; why can't we achieve? The method is correct." The fallacy lies not in the method, not in Buddha, but in this traditional mind. It is not seeing that the whole situation has changed, and every method is organic to a particular situation, and to a particular mind, and to a particular man.

## Kundalini Yoga: Returning to the Roots

Another experience – that of J. Krishnamurti. He will deny method, and to deny method, he will deny Buddha buddhahood too. It is the other aspect of the same coin. If you don't deny Buddha buddhahood, then you cannot deny the method. That is the conformist attitude. If you deny the method then you have to deny Buddha buddhahood also. That is wrong – as wrong as the first extreme.

Extremes are always wrong. You cannot destroy falsehood through an extreme, because another extreme to it will still be a falsehood. It is always in the middle that the truth is. It is neither conformist...and if it is not conformist it cannot be revolutionary. It is always exactly in the middle of two extremes that the truth lies; exactly in the middle is always the transcendental point.

So to me, methods will change. Even a no-method is a method. It may be applicable to somebody. It is possible that to somebody only no method will be a method. In a particular situation even method itself as such will become harmful, but it is always to a particular person; it is never general. And whenever truths are generalized, they become false. Every human being is a particular human being, and no human being is another. So whenever anything is to be used or anything is to be said, it is always addressed to a particular human being: to his situation, to his mind, to him and to no one else.

That too has become a modern difficulty, because in the old days it was a one-to-one relationship – the spiritual search was always one-to-one. It was between a teacher and a disciple; a personal relationship and a personal communication.

Today it is not. It is always impersonal. One has to talk with a crowd, so one has to be general, and truth generalized becomes false. It is always meaningful to a particular person, and I feel it daily, the difficulty. If you come to me and if you ask me something, I answer *you* and no one else. Another time someone else asks me something, and I answer him and no one else. And these two answers may even be contradictory, because these two persons who have asked may be contradictory.

So if I am to be of help to you, I have to be particular. And if I am to be particular, I have to be inconsistent. Only a person who has been talking generally can be consistent, but then truth becomes false. Every statement, to be true, is bound to be an address to a particular person; it is a personal address.

As I see the situation, modern man has changed so much. He needs the new: new methods, new techniques. Of course, the truth is always eternal – it is never new and never old – but the truth is the realization, the end. Means are always relevant or irrelevant to a particular person and to a particular mind, a particular attitude.

Chaotic methods will help the modern mind because the modern mind is itself going chaotic. That – that chaos, that rebelliousness in the modern man – is in fact a rebellion of other centers of the body, of other centers of the being, which have been too suppressed. This rebellion of the modern man is a rebellion of the heart and of the navel against the brain. If you take it in yogic reference the modern rebellion is against the brain.

The brain has usurped the whole territory of the human soul. It has monopolized. It cannot be tolerated further. That's why universities have become the centers of rebellion. It is not accidental. Universities will be the centers of the rebellion in the coming days, because they are the centers of the brain. Universities can be destroyed – that's possible, and is becoming more and more possible – because they are the centers of the brain. In the society the university is the brain; in the body your brain is the university. They correspond. If the whole society is in an organic body, then the university is the head, the brain.

Modern mind is bound to be leaning toward chaos, and chaotic methods will be helpful. They will be helpful in twofold ways. One: they will transform the center of consciousness. And another: they will take rebellion out of you. If my method is used, then a person will never be rebellious, because the cause is fulfilled. He will not destroy the university, because his center of consciousness has gone in. Now he doesn't feel any grudge. He is at ease.

So to me, meditation is not only a salvation for the individual – a transformation for the individual – but of a greater significance. It can be a groundwork for transformation of the whole society, the whole human being as such. Either man will have to commit suicide, or he will have to transform himself.

# 5 / *Esoteric Games: A Hindrance to Growth*

*Osho,*
*Is there a division between body and mind, matter and consciousness, the physical and the spiritual? How can one transcend body and mind to attain spiritual consciousness?*

**The first thing to be understood** is that the division between body and mind is absolutely false. If you begin with that division you will reach nowhere; a false beginning leads nowhere. Nothing can come out of it because every step has its own logic of evolving. The second step will come out of the first, and the third out of the second and so on. There is a logical sequence. So the moment you take the first step, you have chosen everything in a way.

The first step is more important than the last, the beginning is more important than the end, because the end is just an outcome, a growth. But

## Esoteric Games: A Hindrance to Growth

we are always concerned about the end, never with the beginning; always concerned with ends, never with means. The end has become so significant to us that we lose track of the seed, of the beginning. Then we can go on dreaming, but we will never reach the real.

To any seeker, this concept of a divided person, this concept of a dual existence – of body and mind, of the physical and the spiritual – is a false step. Existence is undivided; all divisions are just mental. The very way the mind looks at things creates a duality. It is the prison of the mind that divides.

Mind cannot do otherwise. It is difficult for the mind to conceive of two contradictions as one, of opposite polarities as one. The mind has a compulsion, an obsession, to be consistent. It cannot conceive how light and darkness are one. It is inconsistent, paradoxical.

The mind has to create opposites: God and the Devil, life and death, love and hate. How can you conceive of love and hate as one energy? It is difficult for the mind. So the mind divides, then the difficulty is over: hate is opposite to love, and love is opposite to hate. Now you can be consistent and the mind can be at ease. So division is a convenience of the mind – not a truth, not a reality.

It is convenient to divide yourself into two: the body and you. But the moment you divide, you have taken a wrong step. Unless you come back and change the first step you can wander for lives and lives, and nothing will come of it, because one false step leads to more false steps. So begin with the right beginning. Remember that you and the body are not two, that two is just a convenience. One is enough as far as the existence is concerned.

It is artificial to divide yourself into two. Really, you always feel that you are one, but once you begin to think about it, the problem arises. If your body is hurt, in that very moment you never feel that you are two. You feel that you are one with the body. Only later, when you begin to think about it, do you divide.

In the present moment, there is no division. For example, if someone puts a dagger to your chest, at that moment there is no division. You do not think that he is going to kill your body; you think he is going to kill you. Only later, when it has become part of the memory, can you divide. Now you can look at things, think about them. You can say that the man was going to kill your body. But you cannot say it in the moment itself.

Whenever you feel, you feel oneness. Whenever you think, you begin to divide. Then enmity is created. If you are not the body, a certain struggle develops. The question arises: "Who is the master? The body or me?" Then the ego begins to feel hurt. You begin to suppress the body – and when you suppress the body, you are suppressing yourself; when you fight with the body, you are fighting with yourself. So much confusion is created. It becomes suicidal.

Even if you try, you cannot really suppress your body. How can I suppress my left hand with my right hand? They look like two, but the same energy flows in both. If they were really two, then suppression would be possible – and not only suppression, absolute destruction would be possible – but if the same energy is flowing in both, how can I suppress my left hand? This is just make-believe. I can let my right hand put my left hand down, and I can pretend that my right hand has won, but the next second I can raise my left hand up and there

## Esoteric Games: A Hindrance to Growth

will be nothing to stop it. This is the game we play. It goes on and on. Sometimes you push sex down, and sometimes sex pushes you down. It becomes a vicious circle. You can never suppress sex. You can transform it, but you can never suppress it.

Beginning with a division between you and the body leads to suppression. So if you are for transformation, you should not begin by dividing. Transformation can come only from an understanding of the whole as the whole. Suppression comes from misunderstanding the whole to be the divided parts. If I know that both hands are mine, then the effort to suppress one is absurd. The struggle becomes absurd, because which is to suppress which? Who is to fight whom? If you can feel at ease with your body, you can take a first step that will be the right one. Then division, suppression, will not come.

If you divide yourself from your body, many things will follow automatically. The more you suppress the body, the more frustrated you will be, because suppression is impossible. A momentary truce can be reached, but then you will again be defeated. And the more frustrated you become, the greater the division, the wider the gap that develops between you and the body. You begin to feel more and more inimical to it. You begin to feel that the body is very strong and that is why you are not capable of suppressing it. Then you think, "Now I will have to fight more vigorously!"

That is why I say that everything has its own logic. If you begin with an erroneous premise, you can go on and on to the very end, never reaching anywhere. Every struggle leads you to another struggle. The mind feels, "The body is strong and I am weak. I have to suppress it more." Or it feels, "I have to make my body weak now." All austerities are just efforts to make the body weak. But the weaker you make the body, the weaker you yourself become. The same relative strength is always maintained between you and your body.

The moment you become weak you begin to feel more frustrated, because now you are more easily defeated. And you cannot do anything about it: the weaker you get, the less possibility there is of overcoming the pull of the body and the more you have to fight it.

So the first thing is not to think in terms of division. This division – physical and spiritual, material and mental, consciousness and matter – is just a linguistic fallacy. The whole nonsense is created out of language.

For example, if you say something, I have to say yes or no. We have no neutral attitude. Yes is always absolute; no is also absolute. There is no neutral word in any language. So De Bono has coined a new word, *po*. He says *po* should come to be used as a neutral word. It means: "I have heard your point of view. I say neither yes nor no to it."

Use *po*, and the whole possibility changes. *Po* is an artificial word that De Bono took from hypothesis or possibility or poetry. It is a neutral word with no evaluation in it, with no condemnation, no appreciation, no commitment, neither for nor against. If someone is insulting you, just say "*po*." Then feel the difference inside you. A single word can make so much difference. When you say "*po*," you are saying, "I have heard you. Now I know that this is your attitude toward me. You may be right; you may be wrong. I am not making an evaluation."

Language creates division. Even great thinkers go on creating things linguistically that are not there. If you ask

## Esoteric Games: A Hindrance to Growth

them, "What is mind?" they say, "It is not matter." If you ask them, "What is matter?" they say, "It is not mind." Neither matter nor mind is known. They define matter by mind and define mind by matter. The roots remain unknown. This is absurd, but it is more comforting to us than to say, "I don't know. Nothing is known about it."

When we say, "Mind is not matter," we feel at ease – as if something has been defined. Nothing has been defined. Mind and matter are both unknown, but to say, "I do not know," would be ego-deflating. The moment we divide, we feel we have become masters of things about which we are absolutely ignorant.

Ninety-nine percent of philosophy is created by language. Different languages create different sorts of philosophies, so if you change the language, the philosophy will change. That is why philosophy is not translatable. Science is always translatable, but philosophy is not. And poetry is even more untranslatable because it depends on a particular freshness of language. The moment you change the language, the flavor is lost; the taste is lost. That taste belongs to a particular arrangement of words, a particular use of words. They cannot be translated.

So the first thing to remember is not to begin with division. Only then do you begin rightly. I do not mean to begin with the concept that "I am one." I do not mean that. Then again you begin with a concept. Just begin in ignorance, in humble ignorance, with a basis of "I do not know."

You can say that body and mind are separate, or you can take the opposite position and can say, "I am one. Body and mind are one." But this statement still presupposes a division. You say one, but you are feeling two. You assert oneness against the feeling of two. This assertion is again a subtle suppression.

So do not begin with *advait*, with a non-dual philosophy. Begin with existence, not with concepts. Begin with a deep, non-conceptualized consciousness. That is what I mean by a right beginning. Begin to feel the existential. Do not say one or two; do not say this or that. Begin to feel what is. And you can only feel what is, when the mind is not there, when concepts are not there, when philosophies and doctrines are not there – really, when language is not there. When language is absent, you are in existence. When language is present, you are in the mind.

With a different language, you will have a different mind. There are so many languages – not only linguistically but religiously, politically. A communist who is sitting by my side is not with me at all. He lives in a different language.

Just on the other side of me, someone may be sitting who believes in karma. The communist and this other man cannot meet; no dialogue is possible because they do not know each other's language at all. They may be using the same words, but still they do not know what the other is saying. They live in different universes.

With language, everyone lives in a private universe. Without language, you belong to the common tongue, existence. This is what I mean by meditation: to drop out of the private linguistic world and enter the non-verbal existence.

Those who divide body and mind are always against sex. The reason is that, ordinarily, sex is the only non-verbal, natural experience that we know. Language is not needed at all. If you use language in sex, you cannot go deep in it. So all

## Esoteric Games: A Hindrance to Growth

those who say you are not the body will be against sex, because in sex you are absolutely undivided.

Do not live in a verbal world. Move deeply into existence itself. Use anything, but come back again and again to the level of the non-verbal, the level of consciousness. With trees, with birds, with the sky, the sun, the clouds, the rain – live with the non-verbal existence everywhere. And the more you do it, the more deeply you go into it, the more you will feel a oneness that does not exist in opposition to twoness – a oneness that is not just a joining of two, but is the oneness of the mainland with an island that joins the mainland below the surface of the ocean. The two have always been one. You see them as two because you look only at the surface.

Language is the surface. All types of language – religious, political – are on the surface. When you live with the non-verbal existence, you come to a subtle oneness that is not a mathematical oneness but an existential oneness.

So do not try to play these verbal games: "Body and mind are divided; body and mind are one." Drop them! They are interesting, but useless. They lead nowhere. Even if you find some truth in them, they are only verbal truths. What are you going to learn from them? For thousands of years your mind has played this game, but it is childish; any verbal game is childish. However seriously you play it makes no difference. You can find many things to support your position, many meanings, but it is just a game. As far as day-to-day work is concerned, language is useful, but you cannot move into the deeper realms with it because these realms are non-verbal.

Language is just a game. If you find some associations between the verbal and the non-verbal, the reason is not that you have found some important secret, no. You can find many associations that look important, but they are not really significant. They are there because your mind has unconsciously created them.

The human mind is basically similar everywhere, so everything that develops out of the human mind tends to be similar. For example, the word for mother happens to be similar in every language. Not because there is anything significant about it, but because the sound "ma" is the sound that is most easily uttered by every child. Once the sound is there you can create different words out of it, but a sound is just a sound. The child is just making the sound "ma," but you hear it as a word.

Sometimes a similarity can be found that is just coincidental. *God* is the reverse of *dog*. It's just a coincidence. But we find it meaningful because to us a dog is something low. Then we say that God is the reverse of this. This is our interpretation. It may be that for the opposite of God we created a word *dog* and then gave this name to dogs. The two are not related at all, but if you can create a relationship between them, it appears significant to you.

You can go on creating similarities out of anything. You can create a vast ocean of words, with infinite similarities. For instance, the word *monkey*. You can play with this word and find certain associations, but before Darwin this would have been impossible. Because we now know that man comes from the monkey, we can play word games. We can say monkey as "man-key": the key to man. Other people have joined these two words in a different way. They have said that monkey and man are related because of the mind: man has a monkeyish mind.

So you can create associations and enjoy it, you can feel

## *Esoteric Games: A Hindrance to Growth*

it is a good game, but it is just a game. One must remember that. Otherwise you will lose track of what is real and what is just a game, and you will go mad.

The more deeply you go into words, the more associations you will find. And then, just by tricks and turns, you can create a whole philosophy out of it. Many do that. Even Ramdas has done this, very much. He has played with the word *monkey* in this way; he has compared *dog* and *God* in this way. It is all right; there is nothing wrong in it. What I am saying is this: if you are playing a game and enjoying it, then enjoy it – but never be fooled by it. And you can be fooled. The game can be so engrossing that you will go on with it, and much energy will be wasted.

People think that, because there are so many similarities among languages there must have been an original language out of which all other languages have come. But these similarities are not there because of a common language; they are there because of similarities in the human mind. All over the world, people who are frustrated make the same sounds; people who are in love make the same sounds. A basic similarity among human beings creates a certain similarity in our words also. But don't take it seriously, because then you can lose yourself in it. Even if you find some significant sources it is meaningless, irrelevant. For a spiritual seeker, it is beside the point.

And our minds are such that when we go to seek something we begin with a preconception. If I feel that Mohammedans are bad, then I go on finding things that support my argument and ultimately I prove myself right. Then whenever I meet a Mohammedan I begin to find faults, and no one can say I am wrong because I have proof.

Someone can come to the same individual with a contradictory concept. If "Mohammedan" means being a good man to him, proof of this goodness can be found with this same Mohammedan. Good and bad are not opposites; they exist together. Man has the possibility to be either, so whatever you are looking for in him you will be able to find. In some situations he will be good and in some situations he will be bad. When you judge him, it depends more on your definition than on the situation itself. It depends on how you look at this or that.

If you think smoking is bad, for example, then it becomes bad. If you think that to behave in a particular way is bad, then it becomes bad. If we are sitting here and someone falls asleep while we are talking, if you think it is bad it is bad. But really, nothing is good, nothing is bad. Someone with a different attitude will think that this same thing is good. He will think that if someone lies down and goes to sleep among friends, it is good that he feels the freedom to do it. So it depends on your attitude.

I was reading about some of the experiments that A. S. Neill tried at his school, Summerhill. He experimented with a new type of school where there was total freedom. He was the headmaster, but there was no discipline. One day a teacher was sick, so he told the boys not to create any nuisance to disturb the teacher that night.

But at night, the boys began fighting right next to the sick man's room. Neill went upstairs. When the children heard someone was coming they became silent and began studying. Neill looked into the room through the window. One boy, who had been pretending to get ready for bed, looked up and saw him at the window. He said to the others,

## Esoteric Games: A Hindrance to Growth

"It's no one but Neill. Come on, there's no need to stop. It's only Neill." So they began to fight again. And Neill was the headmaster!

Neill wrote, "I was so happy that they were so unafraid of me that they were able to say, 'There is no need to worry. It's only Neill.'" He felt good about it, but no other headmaster would have felt good – no other headmaster, never in history!

So it depends on you, on how you define things. Neill felt it as love but, again, that is his definition. We always find what we are looking for. You can find anything in the world if you are seriously in search of it.

So do not begin with a mind fixed on finding something. Just begin! An inquiring mind does not mean to be in search of anything but simply to be searching; simply searching, with no preconceived notions, with nothing definite to find. We find things because we are looking for them.

The meaning of the Biblical story of the Tower of Babel is that the moment you speak, you are divided. The story is not that people began to speak different languages but that they began to speak at all. The moment you speak, confusion is there. The moment you utter something, you are divided. Only silence is one.

Many people have wasted their lives seeking things. When something is taken seriously, you can waste your life very easily. Playing with words is so ego-fulfilling that you can waste your life doing it. Even if it is interesting – a good game, amusing – it is useless for a spiritual seeker. The spiritual search is not a game.

The same game can be played with numbers. You can make connections. You can figure out why there are seven days in the week, seven musical notes, seven spheres, seven bodies. Why is there always seven? Then you can create a philosophy around it, but this philosophy will just be a product of your imagination.

Sometimes things begin in very innocent ways. For example, the way counting began. The only reason there are nine digits is because man has ten fingers. All over the world, the first counting that happened was on the fingers. So ten was the chosen limit. It was enough, because then you can go on repeating. So all over the world there are nine digits.

Once nine has been fixed upon, it becomes difficult to conceive of how to proceed with more than nine digits or less. But less can be used. Nine is only a habit. Leibnitz used only three digits: 1, 2 and 3. Any problem can be solved with three digits as well as nine. Einstein used only two digits: 1 and 2. Then counting becomes: 1, 2, 10, 11… For us, there seems to be a gap of eight, but that gap doesn't exist; it is just in our minds.

We have a fixed attitude that 3 must come after 2. There is no "must." But it becomes confusing to us. We think that 2 plus 2 is always 4, but there is no inherent necessity in it. If you use a two-digit system, then 2 plus 2 will be 11. But then 11 and 4 mean the same thing. You can say that two chairs and two chairs are four chairs, or you can say they are eleven chairs, but whatever system you decide to follow, existentially the number of chairs remains the same.

You can find reasons for everything: why there are seven days in a week, why there are twenty-eight days in a woman's menstrual cycle, why there are seven notes in the scale, why there are seven spheres. And some of these things may actually have a reason behind them.

## Esoteric Games: A Hindrance to Growth

For example, the word *menses* means a month. It is possible that man first began counting months according to the menstrual cycle of women, because the natural feminine cycle is a fixed time period: twenty-eight days. This would have been an easy method to know that one month had passed. When your wife begins her menses, one month has gone by.

Or, you can count the months according to the moon. But then the time period that we call one month changes to thirty days. The moon gets bigger for fifteen days and wanes for fifteen days, so in thirty days it has gone through its complete cycle.

We fix the months according to the moon, so we say that a month has thirty days. But if you determine it by Venus or by the menstrual period, it will have twenty-eight days. You can dissolve the disparity by dividing the twenty-eight day cycle and thinking in terms of a seven-day week. Then, once this division becomes fixed in the mind, other things follow automatically. That is what I mean: everything has its own logic. Once you have a seven-day week you can find many other patterns of seven, and seven becomes a significant number, a magical number. It is not. Either the whole life is magical or nothing is. It becomes just a game for the imagination.

You can play with these things, and there will be many coincidences. The world is so big, so infinite, so many things are happening every second, that there are bound to be coincidences. The coincidences begin to add up, and finally you have created so long a list that you are convinced by it. Then you wonder, "Why is there always seven? There must be some mystery to it." The mystery is only that your mind sees the coincidences and tries to interpret them in a logical way.

Gurdjieff said that man is food for the moon. This is perfectly logical. It shows the foolishness of logic. Everything in life is good for something else, so Gurdjieff came upon a very inventive idea: that man must also be food for something. Then, "What is man food for?" becomes a logical question to ask.

The sun cannot be the eater of man because the sun's rays are food for other things, for plants. Man would then be on a lower rung than other species. But this cannot be so because man is the highest animal – according to himself – so man cannot be food for the sun.

The moon is related to us in a subtle way, but not in the way Gurdjieff said. It is subtly related to women's menstrual periods. It is related to the tide, to the ebb and flow of the sea. More people seem to go mad on the full moon. That is where the word *lunatic* comes from: *lunar*, the moon.

The moon has always hypnotized man's mind. Gurdjieff said, "Man must be food for the moon, because food can be easily hypnotized by the eater." Animals, snakes in particular, first hypnotize their victims. They become so paralyzed that they can be eaten. This is another coincidence that Gurdjieff played with. Poets, lunatics, aesthetes, thinkers, are all hypnotized by the moon. Something must be there. Man must be a food.

You can play with this idea. With a fertile mind like Gurdjieff's, things go on falling into a logical pattern. Gurdjieff was a genius who could put things in such a way that they appeared to be logical, rational, meaningful, no matter how absurd they were. He postulated this theory and then his imagination was able to find many connections, many proofs.

Every system maker uses logic to distort, to prove his

point. Every system maker! Those who want to remain with the truth cannot create systems. For example, I could never create a system because, to me, the very effort is wrong. I can only be fragmentary in what I say, incomplete. There will be gaps, unbridgeable ones. With me, you will have to jump from one point to the next.

A system can be created very easily because the gaps can be filled in by the imagination. Then the whole thing becomes very clean and neat, logical. But as it becomes logical, it moves further and further away from the existential source.

The more you know, the more you feel that there are gaps that cannot be filled. Existence can never be consistent, never. A system needs to be consistent, but existence itself is never consistent. So no system can ever explain it.

Wherever man has created systems to explain existence – in India, in Greece, in China – he has created games. If you accept the first step as true, then the whole system works perfectly, but if you don't accept the first step, the whole edifice falls down. The whole edifice is an exercise in imagination. It is good, poetic, beautiful, but once a system insists that its version of existence is the absolute truth, it becomes violent and destructive. These systems of truth are poetries. They are beautiful, but they are just poetry. Many gaps have been filled in by the imagination.

Gurdjieff was indicating certain fragments of the truth, but because it is not so easy to rest a theory on one or two fragments, he assembled many fragments. Then he tried to make those fragments into a coherent system. He began to fill in the gaps. But the more the gaps are filled in, the more the reality is lost. And ultimately, the whole system falls because of those filled in gaps.

One who is enchanted with the personality of a teacher may not become aware of the gaps in his theory, while those who are not enchanted will see only the gaps and not the fragments of truth. For his followers, Buddha is a buddha, an enlightened one – but for others he creates confusion because they see only the gaps. If you join all the gaps together it becomes destructive, but if you join all the fragments of truth together, it can become a foundation for your transformation.

Truth is bound to be fragmentary. It is so infinite that with a finite mind you can never get to the whole. And if you insist on trying to get to the whole, you will lose your mind, you will transcend your mind. But if you create a system, you will never lose your mind, because then your mind fills in the gaps. The system becomes neat and clean; it becomes impressive, rational, understandable, but never anything more. And something more is needed: the force, the energy to transform you. But that force can come only through fragmentary glimpses.

Mind creates so many systems, so many methods. It thinks, "If I drop out of the life I am leading, something deeper will be found." This is absurd. But the mind goes on thinking that somewhere in Tibet, somewhere in Meru Parvat, somewhere, the "real thing" must be happening. The heart is in conflict: how to go there? How to come in contact with the masters who are working there? The mind is always looking for something somewhere else, never for something here and now. The mind is never here. And each theory attracts people: "On Meru Mountain, the real thing is happening right now! Go there, be in contact with the masters there, and you will be transformed."

## *Esoteric Games: A Hindrance to Growth*

Don't be a victim to such things. Even if they have some basis, don't fall for them. Someone may be telling you something that is real, but the reason for your attraction is wrong. The real is here and now; it is with you now. Just work on yourself. Even when one has gone to every Meru Mountain, one has to come back to oneself. Ultimately, one finds that Meru Mountain is here, Tibet is here: "Here, inside me. And I have been wandering and wandering everywhere."

The more rational the system, the more it falls apart, and something irrational must be introduced. But the moment you introduce the irrational element, the mind begins to shatter. So do not worry about systems. Just take a jump into the here and now.

# 6/ *The Psychology of Dreams*

*Osho,*
*What are the different types of dreams?*

**There are so many types of dreams.** We have seven bodies and each body has its own type of dream. The physical body creates its own dream – if your stomach is upset, then a particular type of dream is created. If you are unhealthy, if you are feverish, then the physical body creates its own type of dream. One thing is certain: that the dream is created out of some disease, out of some *dis*-ease.

Physical disease creates its own realm of dreams, so a physical dream can even be stimulated from the outside. You are sleeping; if a wet cloth is put around your legs, you will begin to dream. You may dream that you are crossing a river. If a pillow is put on your chest, you will begin to dream. You may dream that someone is sitting on you, or a stone has fallen on you. These

## The Psychology of Dreams

dreams are through the physical body.

We have seven bodies – the physical, the etheric, the astral, the mental, the spiritual, the cosmic, and the nirvanic – so there is the possibility of seven types of dreams. The second body – the etheric body – dreams in its own way. Those dreams cannot be understood through the physiology – they cannot be understood. And those exact dreams have created much puzzlement in the psychologies of today – in either Freudian analysis, or in Adlerian, or in Jungian. Those etheric dreams have created so many puzzles and problems.

Freud understands them as suppressed desires. There are dreams which belong to suppressed desires, but they too belong to the first body, the physical. If you have been suppressing physical desires – if you have fasted for instance, then in the dream there is every possibility of some breakfast. If you have suppressed sex, there is every possibility of sexual fantasies. But these two belong to the first body. The second, the etheric body, is left out of these psychological investigations, or it is interpreted as physiological.

The etheric body can travel in dreams. There is every possibility of it going out of your physical body. But when you remember it, it is remembered as a dream. It is not a dream in the same sense as the physiological body dreams. The etheric body can go out of you when you are asleep. Your physiological body will be here, but your etheric body will go out and travel in space. There is no time and space binding for it; there is no question of distance for it. Those who don't understand it may say that this is the realm of the unconscious, because they divide man's mind into conscious and unconscious. The physiological dreaming becomes conscious; the etheric dreaming becomes unconscious.

The etheric dreaming is not unconscious. It is as conscious as the physiological dreaming is, but conscious on another level, on another plane. So if you can become conscious of your etheric body, the dreaming concerned with that realm becomes conscious.

And as physiological dreams can be created from the outside, etheric dreams can also be created, stimulated. And there are methods: mantra is one which can create etheric visions – they are etheric dreams. A particular mantra, a particular arrangement of sound, can create etheric dreams. A particular *nada* – a particular word – repeatedly, repeatedly sounded in the etheric center can create etheric dreams. So gurus revealing themselves before their disciples is nothing but etheric travel, etheric dreaming.

There are so many methods. Sound is one of them; perfume is another. Sufis have used perfume to create etheric visions. Mohammed was very fond of perfume. A particular perfume can create a particular dream.

Color can be of help. Leadbeater once dreamed an etheric dream of blueness – just blue, but of a particular shade. He began to search for that particular blue, the color, all over the world; that particular blue was searched for all over the markets of the world. And after years of search, it was found in an Italian shop – a velvet of that particular shade. That velvet was used to create etheric dreams in others also.

The aura of the body…everybody has a particular aura, and the color of it comes from the etheric realm. When someone goes deep in meditation and sees colors and colors and colors, and perfumes and sounds and music absolutely unknown, these too are dreams, dreams of the etheric body. But because we have only searched within the mind on one

## The Psychology of Dreams

level of existence, the physiological, these dreams have either been interpreted in the language of the physiological or discarded, or neglected – or absolutely put into the unconscious.

To put anything into the unconscious is really to deny it, that we don't know anything about it – that esoterical trick of escape. Nothing is unconscious, but everything conscious in the deeper level, is unconscious for the previous one. For the physical, the etheric is unconscious; for the etheric, the astral is unconscious; for the astral, the mental is unconscious. "Conscious" means that which is known. "Unconscious" means that which is still not known, the unknown one.

The so-called "spiritual vision" is of the etheric: etheric dreaming. That is why…they are astral dreams: in your astral dreaming you go into your previous lives. That is your third dimension of dreaming. You can go into your past birth. Sometimes in the ordinary dream, there may be a part of the etheric or a part of the astral. Then the dream becomes a muddle, a mess; then you cannot understand it. Then it becomes impossible to understand because your seven bodies are simultaneously in existence, and something of another realm can pass through the barriers of another, can penetrate into it, can trespass it. Sometimes, even in ordinary dreams, there are fragments of the etheric or astral. Ordinary dreams too: something penetrates things which are not of the physiological.

In the astral dreams, the third body, you can travel not only in space but in time. In the first, the physiological, you can neither travel in space nor in time. You are confined to your physical state and to your particular time – say in the night, ten o'clock. This ten o'clock becomes definitive, in this particular room, and in the physiological space that you have occupied. You can dream in it, but not beyond it. In the etheric, the second body, you can travel in space but not in time. You can be sleeping here and be in space – this is travel in space, but not in time. The time is ten o'clock in the night, still. In the third, the astral body, you can trespass the barriers of time – but only toward the past, not toward the future. The astral mind can go into the past, into the whole series of it, the infinite series, from amoeba to man – the whole process.

This astral mind has been interpreted in Jung's psychology as the collective unconscious. The first is known as the conscious in psychology, the second as unconscious, the third as the collective unconscious. It is not the collective unconscious; it is your individual history of births. Sometimes it penetrates into the ordinary dreams, more in pathological states than in healthy states. A man who is mentally diseased, his boundaries are shaken. He's become fluid. These three bodies lose their ordinary distinctions in a pathological state. So a pathological person, a person suffering from any mental disease, ordinarily can dream about his previous births, but no one will believe him. He himself will not believe it. He will say this is dreaming.

This is not dreaming in the first sense. This is astral dreaming. And astral dreaming has much meaning, it has much significance. But the third body can dream only in the past. It can have visions of all that has been, but not about that which is to be.

The fourth body is the mental. It travels both ways. It is not one way. It can travel into the past, it can travel into the future. This mental body can sometimes dream about the future; in some acute emergencies an ordinary person can have a picture, can have a glimpse into the future. Someone near and dear, someone beloved to you, is dying. This is such an acute state of emergency that the message may be delivered to you in your ordinary dreaming, because you don't know any other dimension of dreaming – you don't know the other possibilities – so the message will penetrate in the ordinary dreaming.

But it will not be clear because there are barriers to be passed and each barrier cuts off something, each barrier transforms something, and each type of mind has its own symbology. So every time a dream passes from one body to another it has to be translated into the symbology of the other. Everything becomes confused.

If you dream clear-cutly, as in the fourth body dream – not through other bodies but through the fourth – then you can penetrate into the future. But only on your own. This, too, is still the individual penetrating into his own future; you cannot penetrate into other's futures.

Now for the fourth body there is no time, because past is as much present as future is present. So the distinction loses meaning. Past, future and present: they become one. Everything becomes a *now*: now penetrating backwards, now penetrating forwards. There is no past and no future, but still there is time. Time as "present" is still a flowing of time. Still, you will have to focus your mind. You can see toward the past, but this will be a focus, and the future and the present will be in abeyance. They will not be before you. When you focus toward the future, the other two will be absent. There will be a sequence. You cannot see the whole as one. Time will be, but no past, present and future as such. And this will be your individual dreaming state.

The fifth body crosses the realm of the individual – the spiritual body. It crosses the realm of time. Now you are in eternity and the dreams have another realm, another dimension. This dimension is not concerned with you as such, but with consciousness as such. It becomes collective as far as consciousness is concerned. Now you know the whole past of consciousness, but not the future; the *whole* past of consciousness.

Through this fifth body, all the myths of creation have been developed. Through this fifth dreaming…the myths of creation. They are all the same. Symbols differ, stories differ a bit, but in the Christian or Hindu or Jewish or Egyptian traditions, the myth of creation – how the world was created, how it came into existence – they all have a parallel similarity: an undercurrent of similarity then in all of them. Through this fifth mind and through its dreaming, this glimpse – through this dreaming, this glimpse. These stories of the great flood…all over the world! No one has "known" them, they are prehistoric. There is no record of them. But still there is a record and that record belongs to the fifth mind, the spiritual body. That mind can dream about them.

And the more you penetrate inward, the dream becomes nearer and nearer to reality. The physiological dreaming is not so real. It has got its reality, but not so real. The etheric dreaming is much more real, the astral is still much more, the mental approximates the real, and in the fifth body you become authentically realistic in your dreaming. Now there is a way of knowing reality. Still to call it "dreaming" is not adequate, but it is dreaming because the real is not present objectively. It comes as subjective experience, but it has got its own objectivity.

*The Psychology of Dreams*

Two persons who have realized the fifth body can dream simultaneously, which is not possible up to the fourth. You will dream privately, I will dream privately, and there is no way of dreaming a common dream. We cannot be communal in a dream up to the fourth, but from the fifth body a dream can be dreamed by so many people simultaneously. That's how they become in a way objective. We can compare our dreams in the fifth; we can compare our notes. And that's how so many people dreamed into the fifth body and all came to the same certain myths. These myths were not created by single individuals – the myths of creation, the great flood, etcetera. They were created by particular schools, particular traditions, particular groups working together.

The fifth body type of dream becomes in a way much more real, amazingly. The four preceding dreams are unreal in a sense, because first, they are individual. Secondly, there is no possibility of another being present in your dream. There is no possibility of sharing the experience; there is no possibility of judging the validity of it – whether it is still a fantasy. And there is a difference between fantasy and dreams. Fantasy means something you have projected; dream means something which is not in existence – you have come to know it. So the more inward, the dreaming becomes less fantastic, less imaginary; more objective, more real, more authentic.

The fifth body has created all the theological concepts. They differ in their language, terminology, formulation, conceptualization, but basically they are one and the same – and dreamed by the fifth center, by the fifth body, by the fifth dimension of dreaming.

Then the sixth, the cosmic body. Now you cross the threshold of consciousness. The unconscious, the conscious, matter, the mind, lose all distinctions. The sixth – the cosmic body – dreams about the cosmos, not about conscious dreams, not about human beings; not a thing involved. Now you cross the threshold of consciousness. Not that you become unconscious but the unconscious world becomes conscious. Now everything is living and conscious. Even what we call matter is now not matter, but mind.

In the sixth body, dreams of cosmic truths have been realized. These theories of Brahman, maya, these theories of oneness, theories of the infinite, these have all been realized in the sixth type of dream. Those who have dreamed into the cosmic dimension have been the creators of the great systems. Symbols still differ, but now there is not much difference. The memory becomes non-symbolic. Language becomes an invitation. Language just fingers something, it just touches, but still the language is positive. We have crossed individuality, we have crossed consciousness, we have crossed time and space, but still the language is positive.

The sixth type of mind dreams in terms of being, not in terms of not being; in terms of positive existence, not in terms of non-existence. Still there is a clinging, the existent; still there is a fear of the non-existent. Matter and mind have become one, but not existence and non-existence, not being and non-being. They are still separate. This is the last barrier.

Then there is the seventh body, the *nirvanic*, which crosses the boundary of the positive and jumps into nothingness. The seventh body has its own dreams: dreams of non-existence, dreams of nothingness, dreams of the void. The yes has been left behind, and even the no becomes lazy. Now even the no is not a no; the nothingness is not nothing. Rather, the nothingness is even more infinite, because the

*The Psychology of Dreams*

positive cannot be infinite in a sense. The positive must have boundaries. However we think, howsoever we conceive, the positive implies boundaries. Only the negative is the realm of no boundaries.

So the seventh body has its own dreams. Now there are no symbols, now there are no forms. Now the formless is. There is no sound but the soundless. Now this silence – the dream of silence, total, unending.

These are the seven bodies, and the seven bodies have each got their own dreams. One thing now is to be understood: these seven bodies and their seven dimensions of dreams can become a hindrance to knowing the seven types of realities.

Your physiological body has a way to know the real and has a way to dream about it. When you take your food, this is a reality. But when you dream that you are taking food, this is not a reality. Rather this is a substitute: a substitute for the real food. The physiological body has its own reality and has its own way of dreaming. These are two ways into the physiological. They are very far off, set apart.

The more you go toward the center, these two lines of reality and dreams will come nearer and nearer to each other, just as lines drawn toward the center of any circle come nearer and nearer as you go toward the center. They go far off, far off from each other as you go toward the periphery, to the circumference. Dreaming and reality as far as the physiological body is concerned are apart, set apart, and the distance between them is the longest. So dreams become unreal; the reality is real and the dream becomes unreal. It becomes a fantasy.

But this separation will not be so much in the second body, in the etheric. The real and the dreaming come nearer. To know what is real and what is a dream is still difficult there, more difficult than from the physiological because they come nearer. But still, the difference can be known.

If your etheric travel has been a real travel, you will travel when you are awake. And if it has been a dream you will travel when you are asleep. You must be asleep for dreaming; you must be awake for the real. When you really travel in your etheric body, then you are totally awake. When you travel dreamily you are not awake; you are asleep. To know the difference, one will have to be awakened in his second body.

And there are methods to become aware in your second body. The inner workings of all the methods of *japa*, the technique of repetitive chanting, they disconnect you from the outside world. You are in an inner circle, revolving and revolving and revolving; you need a little leave from it.

If you go into sleep because of this repetition – this constant repetition can create hypnotic sleep – if you go into sleep, then you will dream. But if you can be aware of your *japa* and if this does not create any hypnosis, then you will know the real as far as the etheric is concerned.

In the third body, the astral, the difference between reality and dreaming is still more difficult to know because the lines have come nearer still. The real astral, if you have known the real astral…then you will go beyond the fear of death, because from that point, one knows immortality. But if the astral dreaming is dreaming and not real, then you will be very crippled by the fear of death. That is the distinction point, that is the touchstone: the fear of death.

The person who believes that the soul is immortal and goes on repeating and repeating it, and convincing himself that the soul is real, will not be able to know what is the distinction between astral reality and astral dreaming. One should not believe in it, immortality. One should know it. And before knowing, one must have doubts about it, uncertainties about it. Only then, when the thing can't kill you – is revealed to you – will you know whether you know it or have just projected it into a dream. It will come on you.

If you have taken immortality as a belief and have practiced with it, it may penetrate into your astral mind. Then you will begin to dream, but it will be a dream. If you have no belief as such, but just a thirst to know, to seek – without knowing what is to be sought, without knowing what will be found, without any preconceptions, prejudices – if you are just seeking in the vacuum, then you will know the difference. The people who are under this type of state may just be dreaming in the astral and not knowing the real.

In the fourth body, these two areas become neighbors. And the faces are so alike that they become twins, and there is every possibility of judging one as the other. The mental body can dream as realistically as the real, and there are methods to create these dreams. There are methods: yogic, tantric and others also. A person who is practicing fasting, loneliness, darkness, will create fourth body type of dreams – mental dreams. And they will be so real, more real than the reality that is surrounding us.

If I can see you in my fourth type of dream, you will become faint in comparison to it, because there the mind is in its full creativity – unhindered by any objective means, unhindered by any objective classifications, unhindered by any material boundaries. Now the mind is totally free to create. The poets, the painters – they all live in the fourth type of dreaming. All the arts are produced by the fourth type of dream.

A person who can dream in the fourth realm can become a great artist but not a knower.

In the fourth type of mind, in the fourth body, one must be aware of any type of mental creation. One should not create anything, otherwise it will be created. One should not project anything, otherwise it will be projected. One should not wish for anything, otherwise there is every danger that the wish will be fulfilled. And not only inwardly, even outwardly the wish can be fulfilled. In the fourth body, the mind is so powerful, so crystal clear. That is the last home of the mind. Beyond that, "no mind" begins.

This fourth is the original source of mind, the fourth mind, so you can create anything. One must be aware. One must be constantly aware that there is no wish, there is no imagination, there is no image; no god, no goddess, no guru. Otherwise they all will be created – out of you. You will be the creator! And there are several feelings so blissful that one longs to create them.

This is the last barrier for the *sadhak*. If one crosses this, then he will not face another greater barrier than this. If you are aware, if you are just a witness in the fourth body, then you know the real. Otherwise you go on dreaming. The dreams will be very good; no reality is comparable to them. They will be ecstatic; no ecstasy is comparable to them.

So one has to be aware of ecstasy, of happiness, of blissfulness, and one has to be constantly aware of any type of image. The moment there is an image, the fourth mind will begin to flow into the dream. One image will shift the mind onto the track. You will go on dreaming.

The fourth type of dreaming can only be prevented, can only be discarded, can only cease to be, if you are just a witness. So this, the witnessing, is the point. It makes the difference because if the dream is, then there will be identification. You will be identified with it. Identification is dreaming as far as the fourth body and its dreaming is concerned. Awareness and the witnessing mind is the path toward the real.

In the fifth body there is no difference: the dreaming and the real become one. Every type of duality is cast off. In the fifth, now one may not be aware – there is no question of any awareness. Even if you are unaware, you will be aware of your unawareness. Now dreaming and the real become just reflections. There is a difference but no distinction. Just as I see myself in the mirror, there is no distinction between me and the reflection, but there is a difference. I am the real one and the reflected one is not the real.

The fifth mind, if it has cultivated conceptions, may be in an illusion of knowing itself in the mirror. A person will know himself but through the mirror – not as he is, but as he is reflected. That is the only… In one way, it is even more difficult; in one way it is not so dangerous. Even when you are looking into the mirror, you are looking into yourself. In this sense there is no danger. But in another sense there is much danger. It may be that you are satisfied, and the mirrorlike image has been taken for granted as the real.

As far as the fifth is concerned, there is no danger. But as far as the sixth is concerned, there is danger. If you have seen yourself in the mirror, then you will not cross the boundary of the fifth. You will not go to the sixth body because through mirrors you cannot pass any boundaries. There have been persons who have remained in the fifth – those who say that there are infinite souls and each soul has brought its own individuality. These persons have remained in the fifth, and they have remained because they have known themselves – but not immediately; through a mediocre mirror.

And from where does the mirror come? The mirror comes through cultivation of concepts...through cultivation of concepts: "I am a soul – eternal, immortal. I am a soul beyond death, beyond birth." To conceive of oneself as the soul without knowing it is to create a mirror. And if the mirror is created you will know – but not yourself as you are, yourself as mirrored through your concepts. The difference will only be this: that if this knowledge is through the mirror then it is dreaming and if it is direct, immediate, without any mirror, then it is real.

This is the only difference, but it is a great one – not in relation to the bodies that you have crossed, but in relation to the bodies that are still to be penetrated.

How can one be aware of whether he is dreaming in the fifth body or living the real? There is only one way. One should drop every type of conceptualization, one should drop here every type of scripture, one should take leave here from every type of philosophy. Now no more gurus; otherwise the guru will become a mirror. From here, no more gurus. From here, you are alone, totally alone. No one should be taken as a guide, otherwise the guide will become the mirror.

From now, the aloneness is total and complete. Not loneliness but aloneness. Loneliness is always concerned with others; aloneness is concerned with oneself. I feel lonely when I lack somebody, some companionship. I feel lonely when there is a sense of lack, there is a sense of companionlessness. I feel alone when *I am*.

One should be alone from here, not lonely. One should be alone from here, alone in every dimension: words, concepts, theories, philosophies, doctrines; gurus, scriptures; Christianity, Hinduism; Buddha, Christ, Krishna, Mahavira. Now one should be alone. Otherwise anybody present there will become a mirror. Now Buddha will be a mirror – very dear, but very dangerous.

If you are alone, this will be the touchstone because now there is nothing in which you can be reflected. *Meditation* is the word for the fifth body. Meditation means to be totally alone – aloneness from every type of mentation. It means to be with no mind. If there is any type of mind it will become a mirror and you will be reflected in it. One should now be a no-mind, a no-thinking, a no-contemplation.

In the sixth, now there is not even a difference now. But still, something comes in between. There is no mirror now. The cosmic is. *You* have been lost. You are no more. The dreamer is not but the dream can be without the dreamer. And when there is a dream without the dreamer, it looks like authentic reality. There is no mind, no one to think. Whatever is known is known, and becomes knowledge. Those myths of creation, they come, they float. You are not; things are floating. No one is to judge, no one is to dream.

But a mind which is not, still *is*. A mind which is annihilated still exists – exists not as an individual, but as a cosmic whole. *You* are not, but the Brahman is, so they say this world is a dream of the Brahman, of the sixth body. This whole world, this whole cosmos, is a dream, maya. But not a dream of ours, not of an individual, but of the total. The total is dreaming. You are not, but the total is.

Now the only distinction will be: is it positive? If it is positive it is illusory, it is a dream, because in the ultimate sense only the negative is. In the ultimate sense, when everything has come to the formless, when everything has come to the original source, then everything is and still is not. The positive is the only remaining factor. It must be jumped over.

So if in the sixth body the positive is lost, you will penetrate into the seventh. The real of the sixth…the "real" of the sixth is the door of the seventh. If there is no positive – no myth, no image – then the dream has ceased. Then there is what is: a suchness. Now there is no existant but existence. Things are not, but the source is. The tree is not, but the seed is.

Those who have known, they have called this type of mind "*samadhi* with seed" – *sabeej samadhi*. Everything has been lost; everything has come to the original source, the cosmic seed, the cosmic egg. Everything has come back, but still the seed is. So this is *samadhi sabheej* – with seed. The tree is not, the evolution is not, but the seed is. But from the seed, dreaming is still possible, so even the seed must be destroyed.

In the seventh there is neither dream nor reality. You can only see something real up to the point where dreaming is possible. If there is no possibility of dreams, then neither the real nor the illusory exists, so the seventh is the center. Now dream and the reality have become one. There is no difference. Either you dream of nothingness or you know nothingness, but the nothingness remains the same.

If I dream about you it is illusory. If I see you it is real. But if I dream about your absence or I see your absence, there is no difference. If you dream about the absence of anything, the dream will be the same as the absence itself. Only in terms of something positive is there a real difference, so up to the sixth body there is a difference. In the seventh body only nothingness remains. There is an absence even of the seed. This is *nirbeej samadhi*, seedless *samadhi*.

## The Psychology of Dreams

Now there is no possibility of dreaming.

So there are seven types of dreams and seven types of realities. They penetrate one another. Because of this, there is much confusion. But if you make a distinction between the seven, if you become clear about it, it will be of much help. Psychology is still far away from knowing about dreams. What it knows is only about the physiological, and sometimes the etheric. But the etheric too is interpreted as the physiological.

Jung has penetrated a little deeper than Freud, but his analysis of the human mind is treated as mythological, religious. Still, he has the seed. If Western psychology is to develop, it is through Jung not Freud. Freud was the pioneer, but every pioneer becomes a barrier for further progress, if attachment to his advances becomes an obsession. Even though Freud is now out of date, Western psychology is still obsessed with its Freudian beginning. Freud must now become part of history. Psychology must proceed further.

In America they are trying to learn about dreaming through laboratory methods. There are many dream laboratories, but the methods used are concerned only with the physiological. Yoga, Tantra and other esoteric training must be introduced if the whole world of dreams is to be known. Every type of dream has a parallel type of reality and if the whole maya cannot be known, if the whole world of illusions cannot be known, then it is impossible to know the real. It is only through the illusory that the real can be known.

But do not take what I have said as a theory, a system. Just make it a starting point, and begin to dream with a conscious mind. Only when you become conscious in your dreams can the real be known.

We are not even conscious of our physical body. We remain unaware of it. Only when some part is diseased do we become aware. One must become aware of the body in health. To be aware of the body in disease is just an emergency measure. It is a natural, built-in process. Your mind must be aware when some part of the body is diseased so that it can be taken care of, but the moment it becomes all right again you become sleepy about it.

You must become aware of your own body: its workings, its subtle feelings, its music, its silences. Sometimes the body is silent; sometimes it is noisy; sometimes relaxed. The feeling is so different in each state that it is unfortunate we are not aware of it. When you are going to sleep, there are subtle changes in your body. When you are coming out of sleep in the morning, there are changes again. One must become aware of them.

When you are going to open your eyes in the morning, do not open them right away. When you have become aware that sleep is over, become aware of your body. Do not open your eyes yet. What is going on? A great change is taking place inside. The sleep is leaving you and the awakening is coming. You have seen the morning sun rising, but never your body rising. It has its own beauty. There is a morning in your body and an evening. It is called *sandhya*: the moment of transformation, the moment of change.

When you are going to sleep, silently watch what is happening. The sleep will come, it will be coming – be aware. Only then can you become really aware of your physical body. And the moment you become aware of it, you will know what physiological dreaming is. Then in the morning you will be able to remember what was a physiological

## The Psychology of Dreams

dream and what was not. If you know the inner feelings, the inner needs, the inner rhythms of your body, then when they are reflected in your dreams you will be able to understand the language.

We have not understood the language of our own bodies. The body has its own wisdom. It has thousands and thousands of years of experience. My body has the experience of my father and mother, and their father and mother and so on – centuries and centuries during which the seed of my body has developed into what it is. It has its own language. One must first understand it. When you understand it, you will know what a physiological dream is. And then, in the morning you can separate the physiological dreams from the non-physiological dreams.

Only then does a new possibility open up: to be aware of your etheric body. Only then, not before. You become more subtle; you can experience more subtle levels of sounds, perfumes, lights. Then when you walk, you know that the physiological body is walking; the etheric body is not walking. The difference is crystal clear. You are eating. The physical body is eating, not the etheric body. There are etheric thirsts, etheric hungers, etheric longings, but these things can only be seen when the physical body is known completely. Then by and by, the other bodies will become known.

Dreaming is one of the greatest subjects. It is still undiscovered, unknown, hidden. It is part of the secret knowledge. But now the moment has come when everything that is secret must be made open. Everything that was hidden up till now must not be hidden any longer or it may prove dangerous.

In the past it was necessary for some things to remain

secret, because knowledge in the hands of the ignorant can be dangerous. This is what is happening with scientific knowledge in the West. Now scientists are aware of the crisis and they want to create secret sciences. Nuclear weapons should not have been made known to politicians. Further discoveries must remain unknown. We must wait for the time when man becomes so capable that the knowledge can be made open and it will not be dangerous.

Similarly, in the realm of the spiritual, much was known in the East. But if it fell into the hands of ignorant people it would prove dangerous, so the key was hidden. The knowledge was made secret, esoteric. It was passed on from person to person very guardedly. But now, because of scientific progress, the moment has come for it to be made open. Science will prove dangerous if spiritual, esoteric truths still remain unknown. They must be made open so that spiritual knowledge will be able to keep pace with scientific knowledge.

Dreaming is one of the greatest esoteric realms. I have said something about it so that you can begin to be aware, but I have not told you the whole science. It is neither necessary nor helpful. I have left gaps. If you go in, these gaps will be filled automatically. What I have said is simply the outer layer. It is not enough for you to be able to make a theory about it, but enough for you to begin.

# 7 / Transcending the Seven Bodies

*Osho,*
*You have said we have seven bodies: an etheric body, a mental body and so on. Sometimes it is difficult to adjust the Indian language to the terms of Western psychology. We have no theories for this in Western thought, but I recognized and have experienced some of these bodies as you explained yesterday.*
*How we can translate these different bodies into our own language? The spiritual is no problem; but the etheric, the astral?*

**You can translate them.** The West has not searched in that direction, but Western mysticism has words, terms for it. Jung is better than Freud as far as the search beyond the superficial consciousness is concerned. But Jung too is just a beginning. You can have a glimpse from Steiner's

Anthroposophy – a German thinker – and a glimpse from the Theosophical writings. That is, Blavatsky's *The Secret Doctrine, Isis Unveiled* and others. Something, too, can be glimpsed from Annie Besant, Leadbeater, Colonel Alcott; then from the Rosicrucian doctrines; then there is a great tradition in the West of Hermes, the thrice-great Hermetic doctrines. There is another secret tradition concerned with the ancient Essenes – that is the teachers of Christ; from there Christ was initiated. And recently, Gurdjieff can be of help, P. D. Ouspensky. ...Something in fragments, and those fragments can be put together.

And your own experience can be of much help. I have also spoken in your terminology. I have only used one word which is not in Western languages: the seventh, the *nirvanic* body. The other six – the physical, the etheric, the astral, the mental, the spiritual and the cosmic – these six words are not Indian. Only one, the seventh, *nirvanic*, is Indian, because in the West the seventh has never been talked about. It is not because there were not persons who knew about it, but because the seventh is something which is impossible to communicate.

If you find it difficult, then you can simply use "the first body," "the second," "the third," "the fourth," "the fifth," "the seventh." Don't use any term. Just use first, second, third, fourth – and describe them. The description will be the right thing, terminology is of no consequence.

These seven bodies can be approached from so many directions. And as far as dreaming is concerned, Freudian, Jungian and Adlerian terms can be used. What they know as the conscious, what they designate as the conscious, is the first body. The unconscious is the second – not exactly the same, but nearer to it. What they call the "collective unconscious" is the third body – not exactly the same, but something approximating to it.

And if there are no common terms in usage, new terms can be coined. That is always better because new terms have no old connotations. So when a newly-coined term is used, because of no previous association, it becomes more significant and is understood more deeply. One is not in the state of mind which already knows. When something unknown, esoteric in meaning, is used then it penetrates our habitual mind much more deeply. So you can coin new words.

The etheric means that which is concerned with the sky, space. The astral means the minutest, the *sukshma*, the last one, the atomic, beyond which matter ceases to exist. For the mental there is no difficulty. For the spiritual too there is no difficulty. For the cosmic too.

Then you have the seventh, the *nirvanic*. It will be better to understand what nirvana means. Nirvana means total cessation, the absolute zero, not even the seed; everything has ceased. The word linguistically means the going out of the flame; the flame gone out, the light put off. You cannot ask where it has gone. It has just ceased to be.

*Nirvana* means the flame which has gone out. Now it is nowhere, or everywhere. It has no particular point of existence and no particular time-moment of existence. Now it *is* the space and the time. It *is* the existence or the non-existence; now it makes no difference. You can use both terms, because it is everywhere – it is everywhere or it is nowhere. To be *some*where it cannot be everywhere, and to be everywhere it cannot be *some*where. Nowhere and everywhere mean the same. For the seventh you can use *nirvanic* because there is no better word for it, and if you stay in your own experiences and they convey to you something parallel to it, then it becomes more easy. Because if you have not known anything, and you have only the words, vacant, empty, without any meaning…words have no meaning at all. Only experience has meaning.

And if there is experience behind the word, the word becomes meaningful – otherwise it is meaningless and absurd. It appears to have meaning even when there is no experience, but that is only an appearance – a linguistic fallacy. So when you have experienced something of it, then you can make that experience deeper, and there are methods that can be used on particular planes.

Begin from the physical, and then every further step is opened to you. The moment you work on the first, you have glimpses of the second. So begin from the physical. Be aware of it, aware every moment, moment to moment, and not only outwardly – because we can become aware of our own body as seen from the outside.

I see my hand. I can become aware of it as I have seen it from the outside, but there is an inner feeling of my hand when I close my eyes too. Now the hand is not seen but there is the feeling, the inner feeling of there being something. So don't be aware of your body as seen from the outside. This cannot lead you inward. If you become aware of your body as seen from the outside, then you can never grow with it, because the inner feeling is quite different.

When you feel it from within, what it is to be inside the body… I can see a house from the outside, it is one thing; from the inside, it is something else. It is the same house but from the inside it is something else. And from inside…

the great difference is that when you see it only from the outside you cannot know its secrets. You know only the outer boundaries; as it looks to others.

If I see my body from without, I see it as it looks to others also. I have not known it as it is for me. And that point from within can only be known to me, and nobody else can know it. My hand, from the outside – you can see it and I can see it. It has become something objective. When you can participate and share the knowledge with me, then this hand as seen from that direction is not mine. It has become public property. You too can know it as much as I can know it.

Only the moment I see it from within, does it become mine in a way which is unsharable. You cannot know how I feel it from within. Only I can know it. So the body that is known to us is not the body that is ours. It is the body that is objectively known to all. It is the body which a physician can know in a laboratory. It is not the body which only I am entitled to know.

Only the private dimension can lead you inward; the public dimension cannot lead you inward. That is why physiology or psychology, which are observations from without, have not lead us to knowledge of our other inner bodies – because this, the first, is the only body which is shareable. The second is absolutely private. And this physical body, too, as it is from within is not shareable. From without only, from the periphery, is it sharcable.

So that is why so many dilemmas are created. One may feel from within a beauty, which is an inner feeling. He may think himself beautiful and no one else is convinced of it. Then there is a dilemma. Ordinarily everyone sees himself as beautiful; no one sees himself as ugly. We may force on someone, that he is ugly, and if we are collectively agreed upon it, he may agree too. But no one feels ugly from within, because from within the body is always beautiful. The inner feeling is always of beauty.

The outward feeling is not a feeling, but a fashion, a criterion imposed from without. A person who is beautiful in a particular society may be ugly in another. A particular shape of the face may be beautiful in a particular period of history, may not be in another. These are criteria imposed from without, but the innermost feeling is always of beauty.

So if there is no criteria, no outside criteria, then there will be no ugliness – even outwardly. We have a fixed image of beauty and everyone has to be compared to it. That's why there is ugliness and beauty; otherwise not. If we all became blind, then there would be no one ugly. Everyone would be beautiful. No one can say that it would be a loss; it might prove a great benefit.

The feeling of the body from within is the first step, and you can be aware of it in any situation. And in different situations you are not always the same from within either. When you are in love, the inner feeling is different; when you are in hate, the inner feeling is different. So if you ask a buddha he will say, "Love is beauty" – not that…not in our ways of thinking, but in his inner feeling. He knows when he is loving he is beautiful.

The inner feeling of the body is of beauty. When there is hatred, when there is anger, when there is jealousy, then something happens inwardly which becomes ugly. You can feel it in different situations, in different moments, in different states of mind.

When you are feeling lazy, then there is a difference. When

you are feeling active, then there is a difference. When you are sleepy, then there is a difference. These differences must be known distinctly. Only then do you become acquainted with the inner life of your body – in disease, in youth, in old age, in childhood. Then you know the inner history, the inner geography. And the moment one becomes aware of his body totally from within, the second body comes into vision automatically.

This second body now will be known from the outside. If you know the first body from the inside, then you will become aware of the second body from the outside as we have known our first body from the outside.

Every body has two dimensions: the outer and the inner. Just like every wall has two aspects – the outward looking and the inward looking – so every body consists of a wall. When you cross the first body and know it from inside, you become aware of the second body from the outside.

You are now in between: inside of the first and outside of the second. From the outside of the first body you can never know the second body. It is the second circle.

This second body, known from outside, is etheric. It is not physical. It is just like condensed smoke. You can pass through it without any hindrance. But it is not transparent; that's why I am using "condensed smoke," not "transparent." You can pass through it without any hindrance, but you cannot look into it from the outside. The first body is neither transparent nor smoky. It is solid. The second body is just like the first one as far as the shape is concerned – just like it, a faint shadow of it.

When the first body dies, the second is not dead. It travels with you. But within thirteen days, it too is dead. It disperses, evaporates. This second body – when you know it while the first body is present, in life, then you can make the distinction clearly.

This second body can go out of your physical body. Sometimes in meditation this second body goes up or down, and you have a feeling that gravitation has no pull over you. Your eyes are closed; you feel you have gone up, you have left the earth. But when you open your eyes, you are on the earth, and you know you were on the earth all the time. The feeling came because of the second body, not because of the first. For the second there is no gravitation. The moment you know it, you feel a certain freedom unknown to the physical, because gravitation is the bondage. A great freedom comes to you from outside. Gravitation is not. You can go outside of your body and come back.

This is the second step: if you want to know your second body from inside, one must have outer body experiences. And the method is not difficult – just wish to be outside and you are outside. The wish is the fulfillment. For the second body there is no effort to be made because there is no pull of gravitation. The difficulty for the first is because of the gravitational force. If I want to come to your house, I will have to fight with the gravitational force. That is why there is effort, labor. But if there is no gravitation, then the simple desire will be enough: the thing will happen.

So, when you come inside your first body and outside of your second, just will, just wait. Only one thing has to be understood: the wish must be total. It must not be antagonistic. It must not have any doubt. It must not be in the shape of "either/or." It must not be "I will be outside,"…made together with "I may not be…." If these two wishes are there they will cancel each other.

The etheric body is the body which is put into work in hypnosis. The first body is not. In hypnotic sleep it is the second body. That's why a person who has eyes becomes blind just by believing the hypnotist when the hypnotist says "You have gone blind." Now he cannot see. It is the second body, the etheric which has been influenced; and the suggestion goes to the etheric.

That's why in hypnosis first you must be in deep trance – only then can your second body be reached. A person who is alright, okay, can be paralyzed by just suggesting to him that he is paralyzed, that "You are paralyzed." The hypnotist must not use any language which creates doubt. Even if he says, "I think it appears that you have gone blind," this will not work. He must be definite, certain, absolutely certain that you are blind. Only then the suggestion works.

In the second body just wish that "I am outside," and you will be outside. Hypnotic trance can be a help. If your first body is asleep, then hypnotic sleep…not ordinary sleep, because in ordinary sleep your first body is still important. The ordinary sleep, the day-to-day sleep, belongs to the first body. It is not of the second. It is just the first body exhausted from the day's labor, work, tension. It is relaxing. In hypnotic sleep, in hypnosis, the second body is put to sleep. And if the second is put to sleep, then you can work with it.

And there are so many things which can work through it, because when you get any disease, seventy-five percent of diseases come from the second body and they spread to the first. Only twenty-five percent of diseases come in the first body and go to the second.

The second body is so suggestible that in every medical college the first year students always become diseased with the same disease...the same disease catches them which is being taught to them. They begin to have symptoms. If the headache is discussed and the symptoms of it, then everybody goes inside, unknowingly, and thinks about the symptoms – whether he has any headache. Because this going inward becomes etheric, suggestions are caught and headaches are created, projected.

The pain of labor, the pain of childbirth, is not of the first body; it is of the second. So through hypnosis, childbirth can become absolutely painless – it is just a suggestion. There are societies which don't feel any type of labor pain, pain of childbirth. It is not in their minds. But every type of civilization creates common suggestions; they become part and parcel of everybody.

Under hypnosis there is no pain. Even surgery can be done – very painful – under hypnosis without any pain. Because the second body...if the second body gets the suggestion that there will be no pain, then there will be no pain. As far as I am concerned, every type of pain and every type of pleasure too, comes from the second body. It spreads only to the first. So if suggestions change, the same thing can become painful, the same thing can become a pleasure – the same thing!

Change the suggestion, change the etheric mind, and everything will be changed, just by wishing totally. When the wish is total it becomes will; that's the only difference. When you have wished totally, completely, with your whole mind, it becomes will; it becomes willpower. And you can go outside of your first body.

When you go outside of the first body then there is the possibility of knowing the second body from within, otherwise not – because when you go outside of it your position changes. Now you are not between the inside of the first and outside of the second. Now you are *inside* the second…because you have gone outside. Now the first body is not.

Now you can behave with the second body from the inside, as you had behaved with your first body. Now be aware of its inner workings, inner parts, the inner mechanisms, the inner lining. Now you can become aware of it. And once outside, then there is no difficulty. Even when you are inside you can become aware of it. The first experience is difficult, after that you will always be within two bodies: the first, the second and you. Your point of attention now will be under two sheets; beyond two circles.

The moment you are inside the second you will be outside of the third: the astral. And as far as the astral is concerned, there is even no need of any will. Just wish. There is no question of totality now. Just a simple wish and you can go inside the third because it is transparent. Even from the outside you can look inside. It is just like a wall of glass – you are outside and you can look inside.

So there is no question even of wishing. If you want to go in you can go. It is as liquid as the second, but transparent also. So this is not a dark smoke, but rather a radiant smoke – a smoke which is just like particles of light. Radiant smoke, transparent. You can go inside – without any wish, you will go. The moment you are outside, you will be inside. You will not know the difference the first time – whether you are outside or inside – because the gap is transparent.

If you work through the first three bodies the fourth body is absolutely wall-less in a way.

## Transcending the Seven Bodies

*What is the size of the third body?*

**The same, the size will be the same.** Size will change only with the sixth body. Up to the fifth the size will be the same. The material, the constant material will change, but the size will be the same up to the fifth body. With the sixth the size will be cosmic. And with the seventh, there will be no size at all, not even cosmic.

Inside the third, the fourth has no wall. It is just a boundary, not even a transparent wall. There is no wall. It is wall-less. So there is no difficulty and no method, no need of it. One who has achieved the third body can achieve the fourth easily.

Beyond the fourth body there is much difficulty, as it was beyond the first, because now the mental realm ceases. The fifth is the spiritual body. There is again a wall, not in the old sense of walls from the first, second... The wall is of dimensions; the wall is of different planes.

These four bodies are four, but concerned with one plane, on one plane. Now you change the story; the plane is different. Before this the division was horizontal. Now the division is vertical. Now the division is as "up, down." Then there is a wall — and a greater one from the fourth to fifth body, because our ways of looking are horizontal.

We look forward, we look backward; our eyes are horizontal, our vision is horizontal. It is not from "down to up." That's why our eyes are placed horizontally, because these eyes are part and parcel of the fourth body, the mental. There is every possibility of a mental blindness: a person whose eyes are completely alright — there is no organic difficulty with them, no organic defect in them — but still a person can go blind. Mental blindness is possible. It happens.

If the mind concentrates its attention, or diverts its attention, eyes go blind. Momentarily we can all go blind. Your home has caught fire: when you are running on the street, someone passes you, you don't see him; he's not seen because your mental attention is somewhere else. The eyes are not working. You see absently; you can see and still you can be blind, because the attention is not behind them. Eyes can be vacant. In fear they become vacant; they see *and* don't see.

From the fourth body to the fifth there is a change of plane. Now in the fourth you are not to look outside and inside, but upward and downward. When you are still in the fourth body you will be looking downward; the mind always looks downward. That's why yoga is against the mind. It is the downward flow, the downward one, just like water. Water goes downward, downward; it is in its intrinsic nature to flow downward. It can never go upward by itself.

So water could never be a symbol of any spiritual system. But fire can be – of so many systems – because fire goes upward. It never goes downward. It has become a symbolic thing. From the fourth to the fifth body, fire is the symbol. One must look upward and one must stop seeing downward.

What will be the method? How to look upward? What is the way?

You must have heard that in meditation eyes should be looking upward, they must be looking to the upward center of *agya* chakra. Eyes must be closed and upward looking, as if you are going to see inside your skull, not downward. Your eyes must penetrate your skull, going upward.

The eyes are only symbolic. The real question is of vision. But our vision, our seeing faculty, is associated with eyes, so the dimension of the eyes becomes the dimension of vision.

## Transcending the Seven Bodies

If your eyes look upward then your vision too goes upward.

In the fourth body – and so many systems begin with the fourth. Raja yoga, etcetera, they all begin from the fourth body. Only hatha yoga begins from the first. Other yogas...they begin from somewhere else. As Theosophy begins from the second, hatha yoga begins from the first. There are systems which begin from the third. Raja yoga begins from the fourth body. This can be chosen and as civilization goes on progressing from the fourth body, so many persons can begin.

If they have worked in their past lives on the first, second, and third, only then, provided they have worked through these first three bodies, only then can the fourth be applicable. So persons who study raja yoga from scriptures or from swamis or from gurus without knowing whether they have worked through their three bodies or not, are bound to be disillusioned somewhere here or somewhere there – because they cannot begin from the fourth. The first three bodies must be crossed, only then the fourth!

And the fourth is the last one where you can begin. One cannot begin from the fifth body; the fourth is the last. So there are four yogas: hatha yoga, the first; raja yoga, the fourth; mantra yoga, the second; and bhakti yoga, the third. These are divisions with the bodies. So in ancient days everybody would begin with the first, but now there are many types of persons. Someone has worked up to the second, someone up to the third; there can be differences. But as far as dreaming is concerned, one must begin from the first. Only then can you know the whole range of it, the whole spectrum of it.

In the fourth body, your consciousness must become like fire – going upward – and this must be checked. For example, in the fourth if the mind goes toward sexuality it is just like water going downward; the center of sex is downward. If it goes into any relationship, the center of relationship – the heart – is downward. Now one must begin looking upward with the eyes, not downward with the eyes.

If consciousness is to go upward, it must begin from the center which is above the eyes, not below the eyes. And there is only one center, there is *agya*, above your two eyes – that which has been known as the third eye. Now the two eyes must look upward toward the third.

This third eye has been remembered in so many ways. In India, a virgin girl and a girl who is married – the distinction between the two is made with a colored mark on the third eye. A virgin cannot look upward. She is bound to look toward the sex center. But the moment she is married she must look upward. Now sexuality must change. Now she must become a mother. Now her journey is toward non-sexuality, or beyond sexuality. She must remember the third eye so a color mark, a *tilak*, is used. Let her remember that now she is not a virgin, she is not just a girl. She must look upward.

There have been *tilaks*, marks on the forehead of so many types: a sannyasin, a worshipper – so many types of color marks. And they too, if possible, with sandalwood, with *chandan*, because this center is a fiery center. It must always be cool. The moment your two eyes look toward the third, a great fire center is created; there is a burning sensation. The third eye is beginning to open, so it must be cooled. Sandalwood is used in India; that was the only thing that could be used at that time.

Still today there is nothing better, for so many reasons; it is cool and with a particular perfume. That perfume too is concerned with the fourth body and the transcendent, that particular perfume...we must have heard that snakes encircle sandalwood trees. The perfume of sandalwood becomes a point of attraction – upward attraction – so the perfume too becomes an upward attraction, a remembrance: the coolness of it, the perfume of it, and the particular place for it.

If you close your eyes – you are not seeing – and I just put my finger at your third eye... I am not touching, my finger is not touching the particular point, still you will begin to feel it. Something will begin to work. This much pressure is enough. Not even the touch, just fingering. Even this much is enough. So the perfume, and the delicate touch of it and the coolness, and the delicate touch of it, is enough. Then your attention is always flowing from your eyes to the third eye point.

So at the fourth body – to cause it – there is only one technique, one method, and that is to look upward. *Shirshasan* was used as a method to do it. *Shirshasan*, the reverse position of the body, was used as a method to reach it because our eyes are ordinarily downward looking. If you stand on your head you will still be looking downward, but now the downward is the upward. Your flow of downwardness will be converted into the flow of upwardness.

So in meditation, without any knowing, some persons will go into the reverse position. They will begin to do *shirshasan* unconsciously, because the flow has changed. And their mind is adjusted, conditioned, to the downward flow. So now this whole thing has become different, unadjusted – they will just go down onto their heads. Now they will feel at ease because they have gained the same position. The downward flow is there – though it is not now downward, it is upward – because as far as the downward and the upward is concerned, it is not to concerned with geographical position; it is upward in relation to your centers.

The *shirshasan* was used as a means of moving from the fourth to the fifth body. The only thing to be remembered and emphasized is looking upward. This can be done in so many ways – with *tratak*, with concentration on the sun, with so many, so many things it can be done. But it is better to do it inwardly. Just close your eyes.

But first, the first four bodies must be crossed. Only then can it be helpful; otherwise not. Otherwise it may prove disturbing. It may create so many sorts of mental diseases because the adjustment of the system will be shattered. The four bodies looking outward, your mind standing outside your first body, and with your inner mind you going upward… There is every possibility that schizophrenia will be the result.

And to me schizophrenia *is* the result of such things. So ordinary psychology cannot go deep into schizophrenia. The schizophrenic has a mind that is simultaneously working in opposite directions: standing outside, looking inside; standing downward, looking upward; standing outside, looking upward.

Your whole system must be in harmony. If you are moving downward you must be outside. That is healthy. Then you are one: a natural unit, a physiological animal, but the adjustment is right. Your outside-based mind must never be tried moving upward – otherwise schizophrenia, division, split personality, will be the result.

Our civilizations and our religions have been the basic cause for the split personality of humanity. They have not looked into the total harmony. There are preachers who are teaching things which are upward to persons who are outside their bodies. These teachings will begin to work with an outside-based person. One part will remain outside his body, a second part will go upward, and there will be an abyss between the two. He will become two persons: sometimes this, sometimes that; Jekyll and Hyde.

There is every possibility that one person can simultaneously become seven persons. Then the split is complete. Then we say there are so many "ghosts" in him. He has himself become seven ghosts. One part is somewhere else, another is somewhere else. One part is clinging to the first body going downward; another part is clinging to the second; another to the third; another going upward; another going somewhere else. He has become a person without a center. Now there is no center in him.

Gurdjieff used to say that such a person is just like a house where the master is absent and every servant claims himself to be the master. Every servant of the house claims himself to be the master. No one can deny him because the master is absent. Anybody can come to that house, knock on the door, and the particular servant who is by chance nearby becomes the master. The person asks, "To whom does this house belong?" The servant says, "To me." Another day, the same person comes. He knocks on the door, another servant is passing by and he claims himself to be the master. Then the guest is at a loss as to whom is the master. The man has become without any center.

We are like that, but still adjusted. The center is dim; the focus is diffused; the master is absent or asleep. And every part of us claims ownership. When there is a sexual urge, sex becomes the master. It is the *proto*, *mono*. It will deny everybody else. Your morality, your family, your religion – everything will be denied. Sex becomes the total master; it is the owner. It will use the house as the owner, not as the servant. And lo, when the sex has gone, and frustration follows it…. And then in frustration, your reason comes up and says, "I am the master. This is nonsense, this is wrong," and it will claim the whole house. It will deny any room for sex. Morality will come back with principles, with teachings, with conditionings. They will claim the house

Everybody claims the house totally. When anger is, you become the anger; anger is the master. Now there is no reason, now there is no consciousness, now there is nothing else. That is the difficulty. We cannot understand persons because of this. A person who is very much loving becomes angry and there is no love, and we are at a loss as to what to understand – whether he is loving or not loving. But the love too was a servant, and anger too is a servant; the master is absent or asleep. So ordinarily, you cannot rely on anybody else because he is not himself; any servant will do. He is not one; he is not a unity.

So what I am saying: the experiment with looking upward must not be done before you have crossed the first four bodies. Otherwise there will be a split which will be impossible, approximately impossible to bridge, and one will have to wait for another life to begin and to start again. So it is better to do it from the beginning, by and by.

If you have achieved – for example, if you have achieved the first three bodies in your past life, you will pass these three in a moment. So there is no difficulty and there is no need to ask from where to begin. Begin from the first; if you have

## Transcending the Seven Bodies

passed any bodies in your previous work then you will pass them again within a moment. There will be no difficulty in passing them again. You know the territory; you know the way. The moment they come before you, you recognize them, you have passed them. Then you can go in. My insistence therefore is begin always from the first – for all!

The fourth body is upward looking and that is the most significant one, because from the fourth you become superhuman. Up to the fourth body you are human. Up to the first you are animal. Only from the second body humanity comes into being, and it comes to flower completely in the fourth body.

Our civilization, the peaks of it, have never gone beyond the fourth. Still, no civilization has gone beyond the fourth body. That is the peak for human beings. Beyond the fourth body is beyond the human being. That is why we cannot classify a Christ: as a human being. A Buddha, a Mahavira, a Krishna: they become something beyond a human – the superhuman.

From the fourth body the upward look is a jump from one realm. When I am looking at my body – the first body from the outside – I am just an animal with a possibility of being human. That is the only difference. I can be compared with an animal: there is every similarity. The only difference is this: that I can be human and an animal cannot. But as far as the situation is concerned, we are both: in the realm of animality, in the realm of below humanity, subhumanity; from the second body, third body, fourth body is the flowering of the human being. So even the fourth looks superhuman to us – it is not.

An Einstein, an Eddison, Rousseau, Voltaire – they look

superhuman. They are not. They are the complete flowering of the human. But we are below human, so they look superhuman. We are below human, they are above us, but not above the human. Only a Buddha, a Christ, a Zarathustra – they cross the boundary of the mind. The mental body is crossed from looking upward.

There are parables worth understanding. Mohammed looking upward, to the sky, says that something has come from above. We take it geographically, so the sky becomes the abode of God. For us, "upward" means the sky; "downward" means hell, below the earth. But the parable, the symbol, has not been understood.

Mohammed looking upward is not looking toward the sky; Mohammed looking upward is looking toward the *agya* chakra. That is the sky for the fourth mind. That is the upward expanse, the sky. And when Mohammed feels that something has come to him from "up," his feeling is right. But upward fire has different meanings.

A Zarathustra looking upward…his every picture is looking upward. His eyes are never downward. Looking upward. And when he first saw the divine there were just flames of fire. The divine came to him as fire. That's why the Persians have been fire worshippers. The feeling of fire comes from the *agya* chakra. When you look upward, you feel the fiery spot – everything burning. Because of that burning, because of that fire, you are transformed. The lower being is burnt, ceases to be, and the upper being is born. That is "passing through fire."

Only up to the fifth body is there any need… From the fifth there is another realm, another dimension. From the first to the fourth body the dimension is from the outside to the inside; from the fourth to fifth body it is from downward to upward; from the fifth it is from ego to non-ego. Now the dimension is different. There is no question of either inside or outside, either upward or downward. It is the question of "I" and "not-I." So the question is now concerned with the center – whether a center or not. I use this word in another connection, to a person without any center.

Up to the fifth body a person is without any center – split into different parts. Only the fifth body has a center; now begins this center. Only for the fifth body is there a center, unity, oneness. But the center becomes the ego; this center will now be a hindrance for further progress. It was a help up to the fifth – and every step which is a help will become a hindrance for further progress. Every bridge, if you have to cross it, you will have to leave it. It was helpful to cross over; it will become a hindrance to cling to it.

Up to the fifth, a center has to be created. Gurdjieff says this fifth center is the "crystallization." This is the crystal. One becomes one. Now there are no servants; the master has taken charge. Now the master is the master – he is awakened; he has come back. Now no servant can say "I am the master." When the master is present, the servant has subsided. They have become silent.

The fifth body is the crystallization. But now for further progress this crystallization must be lost again – lost in another dimension, not lost in this unity, but lost into the void, into the cosmic. And only one who has, can lose. So to talk about egolessness before the fifth body is nonsense. To talk about egolessness before the fifth is absurd. You have not got any ego, so how can you lose it? There are so many egos; every servant has an ego. You are multi-egoistic, a multi-personality, or multi-psychic. There are so many psyches in you.

So when you think of losing the ego you can never lose it, because you have not got it. The first thing to be able to lose it, is to have it. A rich man can renounce his riches, but not a poor one – he has nothing to renounce, nothing to lose. But there are poor persons who are thinking of renunciation. The rich man is afraid of renunciation because he has; the poor man is always ready to renounce because he has not.

The fifth body is the richest. The fifth body is a culmination of all that is possible in the human being as a seed. This is the peak, the fifth: the peak of individuality, the peak of love, the peak of compassion, the peak of everything that is of worth. But now the thorns have been lost; the flowers too must be lost. Then there will be simply perfume, no flowers.

The sixth body is the realm of perfume, the cosmic perfume – no flower, no center. Circumference, but no center – *or* centers everywhere, *or* everything has become a center, *or* now there is no center. There is a diffused feeling. It is not a split. Now there is no division. Even the division of the individual – the "I" and the "not-I," the "I" and "the other" – there is no division.

So the individual can be lost in two ways: one, schizophrenic, splitting into so many persons; another, cosmic, lost into the ultimate, lost into the greater, the greatest, the Brahman, lost into the expanse. Now the flower is not but the perfume is.

And the flower too is a disturbance. When only the perfume is, it is perfect. Now there is no source to it so it cannot die. It is undying. With a source everything will die, with a birth everything will have a death. Now the flower is not, so there is no source. It is uncaused, so there is no death to it and there is no boundary to it. A flower has a limitation; perfume is unlimited. There is no barrier to it. It crosses, it crosses and crosses, and goes beyond.

So from the fifth body the question is not of upward, downward, sideward, inside, outside. The question is concerned with: to be with a center or to be without a center, with an ego or without an ego. That is the most arduous thing to lose. It was not difficult up to the fifth to become concentric, to become a center, because it was ego-fulfilling. Every *sadhak*, every seeker, can go up to the fifth body. It is ego-fulfilling. No one likes to be schizophrenic; everybody would like a crystallized personality – the glory of it, the richness of it, the happiness of it, the very being of it. Everybody likes it.

Now comes a greater question – and not of any method because from the fifth body there is no method. Why? Because every type of method is bound with the ego. The moment you use a method, *you* are strengthened. So those who talk about the fifth and above, they talk of no method; they talk of methodlessness; they talk of no technique; they talk of no "how." Now there is no how. From the fifth body method is lost.

You can go with method up to the fifth body; now method is of no use because the *user* is to be lost. If you use something, the user will be strengthened, positive, become more strong, become even more concentric, become even more solid. It will go on crystallizing, crystallizing, crystallizing; and will become an atomic crystallization. Those who have remained at the fifth body will say that there are so many infinite souls, infinite kinds of spirits.

They are atomists – spiritual atomists, They believe in atoms. Two atoms cannot meet. They have no windows to go to the neighbor; they are windowless, doorless, totally crystallized, lost in oneself; closed to the outside, closed to the upside, closed to everything else.

Egos, windowless. You can use a word of Leibnitz, *monads*. They become monads: windowless atoms. Now there is no neighbor. Now there is no one else. You are alone and alone and alone.

Now one has to lose it. How to lose it when there is no method? How to go beyond it when there is no path? How to cross it when there is no window? How to escape from it when there is no door? The Zen monks have talked about the gateless gate. Now there is no gate, and still one has to go beyond it.

What to do? Don't be identified with this crystallization. Be aware of it. Just be aware of it. Just be aware of this atomic encircling, this ego-lining, this closed house of "I" – just be aware of it. Just be aware and don't do anything – and there is an explosion; you will be beyond.

They have a parable in Zen…

An egg of a goose is put in a bottle, then the goose comes out of the egg and begins to grow. The mouth of the bottle is so small that the goose cannot come out. Now it is growing, growing, growing and growing, and the bottle has become so small that either the bottle has to be destroyed and the goose saved, or the goose will die and the bottle will be saved. And they ask, they ask the seekers: "What is to be done? We don't want to lose either. The goose has to be saved and the bottle also. What to do?"

*Transcending the Seven Bodies*

This is the question of the fifth, the fifth body, when there is no way out and the goose is growing, and the crystallization has become consolidated. What to do now?

They ask meditators to meditate over it. The seeker goes inside a room, closes the door and now he begins to brood over it: what to do? There are only two ways: he'll have to destroy the bottle and save the goose, or let the goose die and save the bottle. There is no other "how," so the mind goes on willing and willing and willing. The seeker will go on thinking and thinking, and will come and suggest something and it will be cancelled because there is no how to it. The teacher will send him back again.

For days and days and nights the seeker, the meditator, is thinking about it, thinking about it, but there is no way to go. A moment comes when thinking ceases. And he comes running and says, "The goose is out! The goose is out!" He comes outside and says, "The goose is out! Eureka! It has been found." Now the teacher never asks "how," because that is nonsense; the goose is out.

From the fifth body, the problem is a koan; it is a puzzle. One should be aware, just aware of the crystallization – and the goose is out. A moment comes when you know you are out; there is no "I." The crystallization has been lost – gained and lost. As a passage, as a bridge, as a path, it was a necessity. To cross the fifth body crystallization was necessary; otherwise the fifth body cannot be crossed. For the fifth the crystallization, the center, the ego, was essential.

There are persons who have achieved the fifth body without going through the fourth. The egoist, a person who has much riches has achieved the fifth body; he is crystallized in a way. A person who has become a president of a country, he is crystallized in a way. A Hitler, a Mussolini – they are crystallized in a way, but the crystallization is in the fifth body and from the fifth body. The first four bodies are not in accordance with it, so it becomes a disease. It becomes a disease. Mahavira and Buddha too are crystallized in a way, but from a different route.

We all long for the ego and to fulfill it, because of the innermost need to reach the fifth body. But if you choose a shortcut, then you will be lost. The shortcut is through riches, through power, through politics. The ego can be achieved, but that is a false crystallization – crystallization not in accordance with your total personality. That is a crystallization like a corn in your foot! Something stony becomes crystallized in your feet and when you walk it pinches – a corn-crystallization.

If the goose is out in the fifth body, you are in the sixth. From the fifth body to the sixth it is the realm of mystery. Up to the fifth, science can be of help; up to the fifth, scientific methods can be used. Or a science can be made about the methods. Yoga is helpful up to the fifth body. From the fifth body yoga is meaningless, because yoga is a method, technique, science.

From the fifth body, Zen is helpful. Zen is very helpful from the fifth.

*And before?*

**And before that yoga is helpful.** Zen, it is not so helpful before. It is a method from the fifth body to the sixth body. Zen...so Zen is a flower. The roots are different. Zen flowered in Japan; it was sown in India. The roots were of yoga; it flowered.

It is from the fifth body to sixth. That's why in the West Zen has appealed so much. Why? It has appealed so much because the West is wrongly crystallized, egoistic. It has come to a particular ego from the wrong sources, not from the four right ones. The ego of the West is crystallized through a wrong process. The West were the masters of the world; they were the owners. They are the richest. They have science, they have technology, they have everything, so they are crystallized. They have the rocket; they can go to the moon. The Western ego is in a sense crystallized.

Zen has become appealing to them but it will not help. It cannot help because the crystallization is wrong. So Gurdjieff is much more helpful to the West because he goes from the first body up to the fifth. He is not helpful beyond the fifth body. Up to the fifth, the crystallization...you can achieve crystallization with him.

Zen will prove just a fashion because there are no roots in the West. It was a long process in the East, a very long process – beginning from hatha yoga and culminating in Buddha. Thousands and thousands of years of humbleness: not of ego, of passivity; not of positive action, of receptivity; not of aggression. It would be better to say a long tradition of a female mind, a receptive mind. The East has been female. The West is male: aggressive, positive. The East has been a receptor, a receptivity. So Zen could be of help because the four processes were working underground – Zen could flower.

Now even in Japan today it has become meaningless,

because Japan is the only country in the East which is now not of the East. It has become Western. Japan was one of the most humble countries, but now the humbleness is just a show. Now it is not the innermost core; it is just a show because it pays to be humble. It succeeds to be humble, the ego gains to be humble. So Zen is uprooted in Japan but seeking roots in the West because…with the help of the false ego, the false crystallization.

From the fifth body to the sixth, Zen is very helpful. But only from the fifth to the sixth, neither the fourth body nor before.

*But is it absolutely useless for the beginning?*

**Absolutely useless;** rather, harmful, rather harmful. Because to talk of the fourth class with the first class, to talk about the university in a primary school is not only useless, it is harmful. It is only from the fifth body to the sixth that it can be of any use. Otherwise it will create satoris, not *samadhis*.

It will create satoris, false *samadhis*, dreams of *samadhi*, and will be used in the fourth body only, the mental body. It will prove artistic, aesthetic. It will create a sense of beauty, it will create a feeling of well-being, but not be crystallization.

Only beyond crystallization will it be useful. The Zen koan, the goose going out without any "how" can only be practiced after many "hows" have been practiced – after so many methods have been practiced. A painter can paint with closed eyes; a painter can paint just as a play. An actor can act just as if he is not acting, and the acting becomes perfect when it doesn't look like acting. But much labor has gone behind it, many years of labor, years of practice. Now the actor has become completely at ease, but that "at-easeness" is not achieved in a day. It has its own methods and its own processes.

We can walk, and we never know how we walk. If someone asks you how you walk you say, "I just walk. There is no 'how' to it." But the "how" has been there when a child begins to walk: he learns. But if an adult talks to a child, saying to him that walking needs no method – "You just walk!" – then it becomes nonsense. The child cannot understand it.

Krishnamurti has been talking in this way, talking with an adult mind to children, saying, "You can walk. You can just walk! The goose is out. Go and walk." And they are listening, and they are enamored, charmed, because it looks easier – it looks the easiest to walk without any method. Then everyone can walk.

Because of this Krishnamurti too has become attractive in the West; because if the West looks to hatha, to bhakti, to mantra, to tantra, to raja yoga, it looks so long, so arduous, so difficult – centuries and centuries of labor, births and births. It cannot be done. Something with speed, a shortcut; something instantaneously instant must be there.

So Krishnamurti pleases them, attracts them. He says, "Just walk. Walk to God. There is no method." When there is no method we think that now there is no difficulty, but no method is the most arduous thing to achieve. To act as if one is not acting, to speak as if one is not speaking, to walk as if one is not walking, effortlessly, is based, rooted on long effort, long labor.

But labor, effort, has a limitation – up to the fifth body. From the fifth body it becomes nonsense. If you go on laboring, if you go on learning, if you go on practicing from the fifth to the sixth body, you will go nowhere. The goose will be in; it will never get out.

This is the difficulty with the yogis of this land. They stick to the fifth body. They find difficulty to cross it because they are method-enchanted, method-hypnotized. They have always worked with method. There has been a clear-cut science, there has been a clear-cut know-how up to the fifth body. It was with ease that they could reach. There was effort – and they could do it! How much intensity was needed – it was no problem to them. They could be intense. How much effort, how much labor was needed – they could supply it. Now in the fifth, they have to cross from the realm of method to no method. Now they are at a loss. They sit down, and this fifth body becomes for so many seekers, the end.

That's why there is talk of five bodies, not of seven. Five seats, five bodies, but not of seven, because those who have gone up to the fifth, they think this is the end. It is not the end. It is still a new beginning. Now again a new beginning: from individual to non-individual. Zen can be helpful, or methods like Zen – no methods – efforts like Zen done effortlessly.

*Zazen* means just sitting and doing nothing. A person who has done much cannot conceive of this, just sitting, doing nothing. It is not conceivable. A Gandhi cannot conceive of it. He has done so much. Just sitting he will say, "Then I will spin my spinning wheel. Something must be done. This is my prayer, this is my meditation." Not doing means nothing. Not doing has its own realm, its own bliss, its own existence, but that is from the fifth body to the sixth body.

## Transcending the Seven Bodies

It cannot be understood before that.

And from the sixth body to the seventh, there is not even no-method. Method is lost in the fifth body, and in the sixth body even no-method is lost. You find someday that you are in the seventh body. Even the cosmos has gone; only nothingness is. It happens. It is a happening from the sixth body to the seventh; this is a happening.


*He chooses…?*

**You can say that,** you can say that, but if you say it then again it becomes of the sixth body. There is neither any chooser nor any choosing. It just happens – uncaused, unknown. Only when it is uncaused does it become discontinuous with the previous body. If it is caused then there is a continuity, then the being cannot be lost. In the seventh body even if you have done something or not done something in the sixth, there is a continuity – the continuity remains. But the seventh body is the total void, the total non-being, the nirvana, the emptiness, the non-existence.

So there is no continuity. There is no possibility of any continuity from existence to non-existence – this is just a jump and uncaused. If it is caused then the cause must lie with the sixth body, and then there is a continuity. So from the sixth body to the seventh it cannot be talked of; from the sixth to the seventh you can have it but not talk about it. It is discontinuity, it is a gap. Something was and something now is – and there is no connection between the two.

Something has just ceased, and something has come in. There is no relationship between the two. One guest has gone from this door, outside, and another guest has come from that side. These two guests are not related: unrelated. There is no relationship between the going of this and the coming of that. There is a gap: unrelated.

The seventh body is the ultimate because now you have crossed even the world of causation – the cause and effect relationship. Now you have gone to the source, the original – that which was before creation and that which will be after annihilation, and that which is always behind; that which is always standing there waiting, waiting, waiting. So from the sixth body to the seventh there is not even no method. They can be of no help here. Here nothing can be a help and everything can be a hindrance. From the cosmic to nothingness there is a happening: happening uncaused, unprepared, unknown, unasked.

This happens spontaneously. Only one thing, negatively, is to be remembered: you must not cling to the sixth body. This clinging will be the negative. There is no positive to go to the seventh but there can be a negative hindrance: you can cling to the sixth body. You can cling to the Brahman, the cosmos, and can say, "I have reached!" So those who have said, "I have reached," they could not go to the seventh body.

Those who say, "I have known," remain in the sixth body. So the Vedant remains in the sixth. Only Buddha crosses the sixth body because he says, "I do not know." To the ultimate questions, he refuses to answer. He says, "I do not know." He says, "No one knows." He says, "No one has known." But he could not be understood.

Those who heard him…they said, "No, our teachers have known. They say Brahman is." But Buddha is talking of the seventh body. No teacher can say he has known about the seventh body – no one can say, because the moment you say it you lose touch with it. And once you have known it, you cannot say it.

Up to the sixth body symbols can be expressive, but there is no symbol for the seventh. It is just an emptiness.

There is a temple in China which is just empty. There is nothing in it: neither any image, nor any scripture – not anything. It is just bare, naked walls. And if you go there and ask the priest – who cannot reside inside the temple, who resides outside; a priest can always be outside this temple, he cannot be inside – if you ask him, "Where is the deity of this temple?" he says, "See!" – and there is emptiness. He will say, "See! Here he is," and there is no one, neither an image nor any scripture: naked, bare, empty temple. "Here! Now!" And you look around, because we look for an object.

If you look for an object then you cannot cross from the sixth body to the seventh. So there are negative preparations. Up to the fifth body there are positive preparations; up, from the sixth body, there are negative preparations. The negative mind is needed, the negative mind which is not longing for anything – not even *moksha*, not even deliverance, not even nirvana; which is not longing for anything, which is not seeking anything, not even the truth; which is not waiting for anything – not even the godliness, the Brahman. He just *is*, without any longing, without any desire, without any wish, without any whim. Just is-ness. Then the happening. Then it happens that he finds even the cosmos has gone.

You can cross into the seventh body, by and by. Begin from the physical body and work through the etheric, then the astral body, then the mental body. You can work up to the fifth body, and from the fifth you must be aware. Doing is not important then; then consciousness is important. From the sixth body to the seventh even consciousness is not important. Only is-ness, the being.

This is the potentiality of our seeds. This is the possibility.

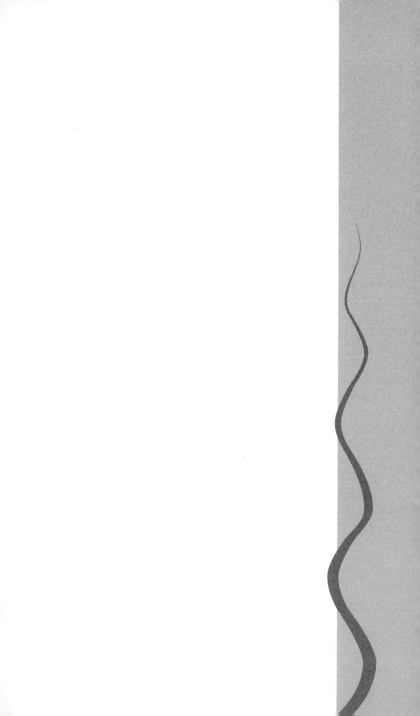

# 8/ *Becoming and Being*

*Osho,*
*Please tell us something about the tensions and relaxation of the seven bodies.*

**The original source of all tension is becoming.** One is always trying to be something; no one is at ease with himself as he is. The being is not accepted, the being is denied, and something else is taken as an ideal to become. So the basic tension is always between that which you are and that which you long to become.

You desire to become something. Tension means that you are not pleased with what you are, and you long to be what you are not. Tension is created between these two. What you desire to become is irrelevant. If you want to become wealthy, famous, powerful, or even if you want to be free, liberated, to be divine, immortal, even if you long for salvation, *moksha*, then too the tension will be there.

## Becoming and Being

Anything that is desired as something to be fulfilled in the future, against you as you are, creates tension. The more impossible the ideal is, the more tension there is bound to be. So a person who is a materialist is ordinarily not so tense as one who is religious, because the religious person is longing for the impossible, for the far-off. The distance is so great that only a great tension can fill the gap.

Tension means a gap between what you are and what you want to be. If the gap is great, the tension will be great. If the gap is small, the tension will be small. And if there is no gap at all, it means you are satisfied with what you are. In other words, you do not long to be anything other than what you are. Then your mind exists in the moment. There is nothing to be tense about; you are at ease with yourself. You are in the Tao. To me, if there is no gap you are religious; you are in the dharma.

The gap can have many layers. If the longing is physical, the tension will be physical. When you seek a particular body, a particular shape – if you long for something other than what you are on a physical level – then there is tension in your physical body. One wants to be more beautiful – now your body becomes tense. This tension begins at your first body, the physiological, but if it is insistent, constant, it may go deeper and spread to the other layers of your being.

If you are longing for psychic powers, then the tension begins at the psychic level and spreads. This spreading is just like when you throw a stone in the lake. It drops at a particular point, but the vibrations created by it will go on spreading into the infinite. So tension may start from any one of your seven bodies, but the original source is always the same: the gap between a state that is and a state that is longed for.

If you have a particular type of mind and you want to change it, transform it – if you want to be more clever, more intelligent – then tension is created. Only if we accept ourselves totally is there no tension. This total acceptance is the miracle, the only miracle. To find a person who has accepted himself totally is the only surprising thing.

Existence itself is non-tense. Tension is always because of hypothetical, non-existential possibilities. In the present there is no tension; tension is always future-oriented. It comes from the imagination. You can imagine yourself as something other than you are. This potential that has been imagined will create tension. So the more imaginative a person is, the more tension is a possibility. Then the imagination has become destructive.

Imagination can also become constructive, creative. If your whole capacity for imagination is focused in the present, in the moment, not in the future, then you can begin to see your existence as poetry. Your imagination is not creating a longing; it is being used in living. This living in the present is beyond tension.

Animals are not tense, trees are not tense, because they do not have the capacity to imagine. They are below tension, not beyond it. Their tension is just a potentiality; it has not become actual. They are evolving. A moment will come when tension will explode in their beings and they will begin to long for the future. It is bound to happen – the imagination becomes active.

The first thing the imagination becomes active about is the future. You create images and because there are no corresponding realities, you go on creating more and more images. But as far as the present is concerned, you cannot ordinarily conceive of the imagination in relation to it. How can you be imaginative in the present? There seems to be no need. This point must be understood.

If you can be consciously present in the present, you will not be living in your imagination. Then the imagination will be free to create within the present itself. Only the right focus is needed. If the imagination is focused on the real, it begins to create. The creation may take any form. If you are a poet, it becomes an explosion of poetry. The poetry will not be a longing for the future, but an expression of the present. Or if you are a painter, the explosion will be of painting. The painting will not be of something as you have imagined it, but as you have known it and lived it.

When you are not living in the imagination, the present moment is given to you. You can express it, or you can go into silence.

But the silence, now, is not a dead silence that is practiced. The silence is also an expression of the present moment. The moment is so deep that now it can be expressed only through silence. Not even poetry is adequate; painting is not adequate. No expression is possible. Silence is the only expression. This silence is not something negative but, rather, a positive flowering. Something has flowered within you, the flower of silence, and through this silence all that you are living is expressed.

A second point is also to be understood: this expression of the present through the imagination is neither an imagination of the future nor a reaction against the past. It is not an expression of any experience that has been known. It is the experience of experiencing — as you are living it, as it is happening in you; not a lived experience, but a living process of experiencing.

Then your experience and experiencing are not two things. They are one and the same. Then there is no painter. The experiencing itself has become the painting; the experiencing itself has expressed itself. You are not a creator; you are creativity, a living energy. You are not a poet; you are poetry. The experience is neither for the future nor for the past; it is neither from the future nor from the past. The moment itself has become eternity, and everything comes from it. It is a flowering.

This flowering will have seven layers, just like tension has seven layers. It will exist in each body. For example, if it happens on the physiological level, you will become beautiful in quite a new sense. This beauty is not of form but of the formless, not of the visible but of the invisible. And if you can feel this non-tense moment in your body, you will know a well-being that you have not known before, a positive well-being.

We have known states of well-being that are negative: negative in the sense that when we are not ill we say we are healthy. This health is simply a negation of disease. It has nothing positive about it; it is just that disease is not there. The medical definition of health is that if you are not ill then you are healthy. But health has a positive dimension also. It is not just the absence of illness; it is the presence of health.

Your body can be non-tense only when you are living a moment-to-moment existence. If you are eating and the moment has become eternity, then there is no past and no future. The very process of eating is all that is. You are not doing something; you have become the doing. There will be no tension; your body will feel fulfilled. Or if you are in sexual communion and the sex is not just a relief from sexual tension but, rather, a positive expression of love – if the moment has become total, whole, and you are in it completely – then you will know a positive well-being in your body.

If you are running, and the running has become the totality of your existence; if you *are* the sensations that are coming to you, not something apart from them but one with them; if there is no future, no goal to this running, running itself is the goal – then you know a positive well-being. Then your body is non-tense. On the physiological level, you have known a moment of non-tense living.

And the same is true with each of the seven bodies. To understand a non-tense moment in the first body is easy because we already know two things that are possible in the body: disease, a positive illness; negatively defined well-being, an absence of illness. This much we have already known, so we can conceive of a third possibility, that of positive well-being, health. But to understand what non-tension is in the second body, the etheric, is a bit more difficult, because you have not known anything about it. Still, certain things can be understood.

Dreams are basically concerned with the second body, the etheric. So ordinarily when we talk about dreams what we are talking about are dreams of the etheric body. But if your physical body has been living in tension, then many dreams will be created by it. For example, if you have been hungry or on a fast, then a particular type of dream is created. This is physiological dreaming. It is not concerned with the etheric body.

The etheric body has its own tension. We know the etheric body only in dreams, so if the etheric body is tense, the dream becomes a nightmare. Now, even in your dream you will be tense; the tension will follow you.

The first tension in the etheric body is concerned with the fulfillment of your desires. We all have dreams about love. Sex is physiological; love is not. Love has nothing to do with the physical body. It is concerned with the etheric body, but if it is not fulfilled then even your physical body may suffer because of it. Not only does your physical body have needs that have to be fulfilled, but your etheric body also has needs. It has its own hungers; it also needs food. Love is that food.

We all go on dreaming about love, but we are never in love. Everybody dreams about love – how it should be, with whom it should be – and everyone is frustrated in it. Either we are dreaming about the future or, in frustration about the past, but we are never loving.

There are other tensions in the etheric body as well, but love is the one that can be most easily understood. If you can love in the moment, then a non-tense situation is created in the etheric body. But you cannot love in the moment if you have demands, expectations, conditions for your love, because demands, expectations and conditions are concerned with the future.

The present is beyond our specifications. It is as it is. But you can have expectations about the future: how it should be. Love too has become a "should" – it is always about what "should be." You can be loving in the present only if your love is not an expectation, a demand; only if it is unconditional.

Also, if you are loving only to one person and not to someone else, then you can never love in the present. If your love is a relationship and not a state of mind, you cannot love in the present because, very subtly, that too is a condition. If I say I can be loving only to you, then when you are not there I will not be loving. For twenty-three hours I will be in a state of not-loving and only for one hour, when I am with you, will I be loving. This is impossible! You cannot be in a state of love one moment and not be in love another moment.

If I am healthy, I am healthy for twenty-four hours. It is impossible to be healthy for one hour and unhealthy for the other twenty-three hours. Health is not a relationship; it is a state of being.

Love is not a relationship between two persons. It is a state of mind within yourself. If you are loving, you are loving to everybody – not only to persons, but to things as well. Love also moves from you to objects. Even when you are alone, when no one is there, you are loving. It is just like breathing. If I take an oath that I will breathe only when I am with you, only death can follow. Breathing is not relationship; it is not tied to any relationship. And for the etheric body, love is just like breathing. It is its breath.

So either you are loving, or you are not loving. The type of love that humanity has created is very dangerous. Even disease has not created as much nonsense as this so-called love has created. The whole of humanity is diseased because of this wrong notion of love.

If you can love and be loving, irrespective of whom, then your second body can have a sense of well-being, a positive at-easeness. Then there are no nightmares. Dreams become a poetry. Then something happens in your second body, and the perfume of it not only pervades you but others also. Wherever you are, the perfume of your love spreads. And of course it has its own response, its own echoing.

Real love is not a function of the ego. The ego is always asking for power, so even when you love – because your love is not real, because it is just a part of the ego – it is bound to be violent. Whenever we love, it is a violence, a type of war. Father and son, mother and daughter, husband and wife – they are not lovers; we have converted them into enemies. They are constantly fighting, and only when they are not fighting do we say it is love. The definition is negative. Between two battles there is a gap, a period of peace.

But really, between two wars there is no possibility of peace. The so-called peace is only a preparation for the coming war. There is no peace between husband and wife, no love. The gap that we call love is only a preparation for the coming fight. We think that there is health when we are between two illnesses, and we think that there is love when we are between two fights. It is not love. It is only a gap between fights. You cannot go on fighting for twenty-four hours, so at some point you begin to love your enemy.

Love is never possible as a relationship but only as a state of mind. If love comes to you as a state of mind, then your second body – the etheric body – becomes at ease, non-tense. It is relaxed. There are other reasons for tension in the second body, but I am talking about the one that can be most easily understood. Because we think we know love, it can be talked about.

The third body is the astral body. It has its own tensions. They are concerned not only with this life but with your previous lives. Tension in the third body is because of the accumulation of everything you have been and of everything you have been longing for. Your total longing, thousands and

## Becoming and Being

thousands of lives and their repetitive longings, are in the astral body. And you have always been longing! It does not matter for what – the longing is there.

The astral body is a storehouse of your total longings, your total desires. That is why it is the most tense part of your being. When you go into meditation you become aware of astral tensions, because meditation starts from the third body. People who have begun to be aware of these tensions through meditation come to me and say, "Since I started meditating, tensions have increased." They have not increased, but now you have become aware of them. Now you know something that you were not aware of before.

These are astral tensions. Because they are essences of so many lives, they cannot be described by any particular word. Nothing can be said about them that can be understood. They can only be lived, and known.

Desiring itself is the tension. We are never without the desire for something or other. There are even people who desire desirelessness. It becomes a total absurdity. In the third body, the astral body, you can desire to be desireless. In fact, the desire to be desireless is one of the strongest desires. It can create one of the biggest gaps between what is and what you want to be.

So accept your desires as they are, and know that you have had so many desires throughout so many lives. You have desired so much, and the whole thing has been accumulated. So for the third body – the astral body – accept your desires as they are. Do not fight with them; do not create a desire against desires. Just accept them. Know that you are full of desires, and be at ease with it. Then you will become non-tense in the astral body.

If you can accept the infinite crowd of desires within you without creating a desire *against* these desires, if you can be in the crowd of desires – they are your whole accumulated past – and accept them as they are, if this acceptance becomes total, then in a single moment the whole crowd disappears. They are no longer there, because they can exist only against a background of desiring, a constant desiring for that which is not.

The object of desire does not matter; it is irrelevant. Desire even desirelessness and the background is there; the whole crowd will be there. If you accept your desire, a moment of desirelessness is created. You accept your desire as it is. Now there is nothing to desire; desiring is not there. You accept everything as it is, even your desires. Then the desires evaporate; nothing has to be done with them. The astral body becomes at ease; it comes to a state of positive well-being. Only then can you proceed to the fourth body.

The fourth body is the mental body. Just as there are desires in the astral body, in the mental body there are thoughts: contradictory thoughts, a whole crowd of them, each thought asserting itself as the whole, each thought possessing you as if it were the whole. So the tension in the fourth body is created by thoughts. Being without thoughts – not asleep, not unconscious, but a thoughtless consciousness – is the health, the well-being of the fourth body. But how can one be conscious and thoughtless?

Every moment, new thoughts are being created. Every moment something of your past is coming into conflict with something of your present. You were a communist and now you are a Catholic and believe in something else, but the past is still there. You can become a Catholic, but you cannot throw

*Becoming and Being*

off your communism. It remains in you. You can change your thoughts, but the discarded thoughts are always there waiting. You cannot unlearn them. They reach into your depths; they go into the unconscious. They will not show themselves to you because you have discarded them, but they will remain there, waiting for their chance. And the chance will come. Even in a period of twenty-four hours, there will be a moment when you will be a communist again and then again you will be a Catholic. This will go on and on, back and forth, and the total effect will be confusion.

So for the mental body, tension means confusion — contradictory thoughts, contradictory experiences, contradictory expectations — and ultimately results in a confused mind. And the confused mind will only become more confused if it tries to go beyond confusion, because out of a state of confusion, no-confusion cannot be achieved.

You are confused. Spiritual seeking will create a new dimension for your confusion. All your other confusions are still there, and now a new confusion has been added. You meet this guru, then that, then the next, and each guru brings new confusion to you. The old confusion will be there, and a new one will be added. You will be a madhouse. This is what happens in the fourth body, the mental body. There, confusion is the tension.

How can one cease to be confused? You can cease to be confused only if you do not deny one particular thought in favor of another, if you do not deny anything — if you do not deny communism in favor of religiousness, if you do not deny God in favor of a philosophy of atheism. If you accept everything that you think, there is no choice to be made and tensions disappear. If you go on choosing, you go on adding to your tensions.

Awareness must be choiceless. You must be aware of your total thought process, the total confusion. The moment you become aware of it, you will know that it is all confusion. Nothing is to be chosen; the whole house must be discarded. Once you know it is just a confusion, the house can be discarded at any time; there is no difficulty in discarding it.

So begin to be aware of your total mind. Do not choose; be choiceless. Do not say, "I am an atheist," or, "I am a theist." Do not say, "I am a Christian," or, "I am a Hindu." Do not choose. Just be aware that sometimes you are an atheist and sometimes a theist, sometimes you are a Christian and sometimes a communist, sometimes a saint and sometimes a sinner. Sometimes one ideology appeals to you and sometimes another, but these are all fads.

Be totally aware of it. The very moment you become aware of the total process of your mind is a moment of nonidentity. Then you are not identified with your mind. For the first time you know yourself as consciousness and not as mind. Mind itself becomes an object to you. Just as you are aware of other people, just as you are aware of the furniture in your house, you become aware of your mind, the mental process. Now you are this awareness – unidentified with the mind.

The difficulty with the fourth body, the mental body, is that we are identified with our minds. If your body becomes ill and someone says you are ill, you do not feel offended; but if your mind becomes ill and someone says, "Your mind is ill; you seem to be going insane," then you are offended. Why?

When someone says, "Your body seems to be ill," you feel that he has sympathized with you. But if someone says something about mental illness – that as far as your mind is

## Becoming and Being

concerned, you seem to be derailed, you are neurotic – then you are offended because there is a deeper identification with the mind than with the body.

You can feel yourself to be separate from the body. You can say, "This is my hand." But you cannot say, "This is my mind," because you think, "My mind means *me*." If I want to operate on your body you will allow me, but you will not allow me to operate on your mind. You will say, "No, this is too much! My freedom will be lost!" Mind is much more deeply identified. It is us. We do not know anything beyond it, so we are identified with it.

We know something beyond the body: the mind. That is why the possibility of being non-identified with the body exists. But we do not know anything beyond the mind. Only if you become aware of thoughts can you come to know that mind is nothing but a process, an accumulation, a mechanism, a storehouse, a computer of your past experiences, your past learning, your past knowledge. It is not you – you can be without it. The mind can be operated on, it can be changed; it can be thrown from you.

And now, there are new possibilities. Someday even your mind will be able to be transplanted into someone else. Just as the heart can be transplanted, sooner or later memory will be able to be transplanted. Then a person who is dying will not die completely. At least his memory can be saved and transplanted into a new child. The child will acquire the whole memory of the person. He will talk about experiences through which he has not passed but he will say, "I have known." Whatever the dead man knew the child will know, because the whole mind of the dead person has been given to him.

This seems dangerous, and it is possible that we will not allow it to happen because our own identity will be lost. We are our minds! But to me, the possibility has much potential. A new humanity may be born out of it. We can be aware of the mind because the mind is not us; it is not "me." My mind is as much a part of my body as my kidney is. Just as I can be given a new kidney and I will still be the same person, with nothing changed, so too I can go on living with a transplanted mind with nothing changed. I can go on being the old self I was, but with a new mind added to me. Mind too is a mechanism. But because of our identification with it, tension is created.

So with the fourth body, awareness is health and unawareness is disease; awareness is non-tension and non-awareness is tension – because of thoughts. Because of your identification with them, you go on living in your thoughts and a barrier is created between you and your existential being.

There is a flower within your reach, but you will never come to know it because you are thinking about it. The flower will die, and you will go on thinking about it. Thinking has created a film between you and the experience – transparent, but not so transparent; only an illusion of transparency.

For example, you are listening to me. But it may be that you are not really listening. If you are thinking about what I am saying, you have ceased listening. Then you have gone ahead or gone back; you are not with me. Either it is the past you will be repeating in your mind or it will be the future projected through the past, but it will not be what I am saying.

It is even possible that you can repeat verbatim what I have said. Your mechanism is recording it. It can repeat what

## Becoming and Being

I have said, reproduce it. Then you will claim, "If I have not heard you, how can I reproduce it?" But a tape recorder does not hear me. Your mind can go on working just like a machine. You may be present, or you may not be. You are not needed. You can go on thinking and still be listening. The mind – the fourth body, the mental body – has become a barrier.

Between you and that which is, there is a barrier. The moment you come to touch, you move away from the experience. The moment you come to look, you move away. I take your hand in my hand. This is an existential thing. But it may be that you are not there. Then you have missed. You have known – you have touched and experienced – but you were in your thoughts.

So at the fourth body one must be aware of one's thought process, taken as a whole – not choosing, not deciding, not judging; just aware of it. If you become aware, you become non-identified. And non-identification with the mechanism of the mind is non-tension.

The fifth body is the spiritual body. As far as the spiritual body is concerned, ignorance of oneself is the only tension. All the time you *are*, you know perfectly well that you do not know yourself. You will pass through life, you will do this and that, you will achieve this and that, but the sense of self-ignorance will be with you continuously. It will be lurking behind you; it will be a constant companion no matter how much you try to forget it, how much you try to escape from it. You cannot escape from your ignorance. You *know* that you don't know. This is the disease at the fifth level.

Those in Delphi who wrote on the temple, "Know thyself," were concerned with the fifth body. They were working on it. Socrates continuously repeated, "Know thyself." He was concerned with the fifth body. For the fifth body, *atmagyana*, self-knowledge, is the only knowledge.

Mahavira said, "By knowing oneself, one knows all." It is not so. One cannot know all by knowing oneself. But the antithesis is correct. By not knowing oneself, one cannot know anything. So to balance this, Mahavira said, "By knowing yourself, you will know all." Even if I know everything, if I do not know myself, what is the use? How can I know the basic, the foundational, the ultimate, if I have not even known myself? It is impossible.

So with the fifth body, the tension is between knowing and ignorance. But remember, I am saying knowing and ignorance; I am not saying knowledge and ignorance. Knowledge can be gathered from scriptures; knowing cannot be gathered from anywhere. There are so many persons operating under this fallacy, this misunderstanding between knowledge and knowing. Knowing is always yours. I cannot transfer my knowing to you; I can only transfer my knowledge. Scriptures communicate knowledge, not knowing. It can say you are divine, you are *atman*, you are the self, but this is not knowing.

If you cling to this knowledge, there will be great tension. Ignorance will be there along with false, acquired knowledge and information – borrowed knowledge. You will be ignorant, but you will feel that you know. Then there is much tension. It is better to be ignorant and know perfectly that "I am an ignorant man." Then tension is there, but it is not so great. If you do not delude yourself with knowledge acquired from others, then you can seek and search within yourself, and knowing is possible.

## Becoming and Being

Because you *are*, this much is certain: that whatever you are, you *are*. This cannot be denied. Another thing: you are someone who knows. It may be that you know others, it may be that you know only illusions, it may be that what you know is not correct, but you know. So two things can be taken for granted: your existence and your consciousness.

But a third thing is lacking. The essential personality of man can be conceived through three dimensions: existence, consciousness and bliss – *sat-chit-anand*. We know that we are existence itself; we know that we are someone who knows – consciousness itself. Only the bliss is lacking. But if you seek inside yourself, you will know the third also. It is there. The blissfulness, the ecstasy of one's existence is there. And when you know it, you will know yourself completely: your existence, your consciousness, your bliss.

You cannot know yourself completely unless bliss is known, because a person who is not blissful will go on escaping from himself. Our whole life is an escape from ourselves. Others are significant to us because they help us to escape. That is why we are all other-oriented. Even if one becomes religious, he creates God as the other. He becomes other-oriented again; the same fallacy is repeated.

So at the fifth stage, one has to be in search of oneself from within. This is not a search, but a "being in search."

Only up to the fifth body are you needed. Beyond the fifth, things become easy and spontaneous. The sixth body is cosmic. The tension is between you – your feelings of individuality, of limitation – and the unlimited cosmos. Even in the fifth stage you will be embodied in your spiritual body. You will be a person. That "person" will be the tension for the sixth. So to achieve a non-tense existence with the cosmos, to be at one with the cosmos, you must cease to be an individual.

Jesus says, "Whoever loses himself will find himself." This statement is concerned with the sixth body. Up to the fifth it cannot be understood, because it is completely anti-mathematical. But from the sixth, this is the only mathematics, the only rational possibility: to lose oneself.

We have been enhancing ourselves, crystallizing ourselves. Up to the fifth body the crystallization, the selfhood, the individuality can be carried. But if someone insists on being an individual, he remains with the fifth. So many spiritual systems stop with the fifth. All those who say that the soul has its own individuality, and the individuality will remain even in a liberated state – that you will be an individual, embodied in your selfhood – any system that says this, stops with the fifth. In such a system, there will be no concept of godliness. It is not needed.

The concept of godliness comes only with the sixth body. Godliness means the cosmic individuality, or, it would be better to say, the cosmic no-individuality. It is not that "I" am in existence; it is the total within me that has made it possible for me to exist. I am just a point, one link among infinite links of existence. If the sun does not rise tomorrow, I will not be. I will go out of existence; the flame will go out. I am here because the sun exists. It is so far away, but still it is linked with me. If the earth dies, as so many planets have died, then I cannot live because my life is one with the life of the earth. Everything exists in a chain of existence. It is not that we are islands. We are the ocean.

At the sixth, the feeling of individuality is the only tension against an oceanic feeling – a feeling without limitation, a

*Becoming and Being*

feeling that is beginningless and endless, a feeling not of "me" but of "we." And the "we" includes everything. Not only persons, not only organic beings, but everything that exists. "We" means the existence itself.

So "I" will be the tension at the sixth. How can you lose the "I," how can you lose your ego? You will not be able to understand right now, but if you achieve the fifth, it will become easy. It is just like a child who is attached to a toy and cannot conceive of how he can throw it away. But the moment childhood is gone, the toy is thrown away. He never goes back to it. Up to the fifth body the ego is very significant, but beyond the fifth it becomes just like a toy that a child has been playing with. You just throw it away; there is no difficulty.

The only difficulty will be if you have achieved the fifth body as a gradual process and not as a sudden enlightenment. Then, to throw the "I" completely in the sixth becomes difficult. So beyond the fifth, all those processes that are sudden become helpful. Before the fifth, gradual processes seem to be easier; but beyond the fifth, they become a hindrance.

So at the sixth, the tension is between individuality and an oceanic consciousness. The drop must lose itself to become the ocean. It is not really losing itself, but from the standpoint of the drop it seems so. On the contrary, the moment drop is lost, the ocean has been gained. It is not really that the drop has lost itself. It has become the ocean now.

The seventh body is the *nirvanic*. The tension in the seventh body is between existence and non-existence. In the sixth, the seeker has lost himself, but not existence. He *is* – not as an individual, but as the cosmic being. Existence is there.

There are philosophies and systems that stop with the sixth. They stop with godliness or with *moksha*: liberation. The seventh means to lose even existence into non-existence. It is not losing oneself; it is just losing. The existential becomes non-existential. Then you come to the original source from which all existence comes and into which it goes. Existence comes out of it; non-existence goes back into it.

Existence itself is just a phase. It must go back. Just as day comes and night follows, just as night goes and day follows, so existence comes and non-existence follows; non-existence comes and existence follows. If one is to know totally, then he must not escape from non-existence. If he is to know the total circle, he must become non-existential.

Even the cosmic is not total, because non-existence is beyond it. So even godliness is not total. Godliness is just part of Brahman; it is not Brahman itself. Brahman means all light and darkness combined, life and death combined, existence and non-existence combined. Godliness is not death; it is only life. Godliness is not non-existence; it is only existence. Godliness is not darkness; it is only light. It is only part of the total being, not the total.

To know the total is to become nothing. Only nothingness can know the wholeness. Wholeness is nothingness, and nothingness is the only wholeness – for the seventh body.

So these are the tensions in the seven bodies, beginning with the physiological. If you understand your physiological tension, the relief of it and the well-being of it, then you can very easily proceed to all seven bodies. The realization of at-easeness in the first body becomes a stepping stone to the second. And if you realize something in the

## Becoming and Being

second – if you feel a non-tense etheric moment – then the step toward the third is taken.

In each body, if you start with well-being, the door to the next body opens automatically. But if you are defeated in the first body it becomes very difficult, even impossible, to open up further doors.

So begin with the first body and do not think of the other six bodies at all. Live in the physical body completely, and you will suddenly know that a new door has opened. Then continue on further. But never think of the other bodies or it will be disturbing and will create tensions.

So whatever I have said – forget it!

# 9/ *The Fallacy of Knowledge*

**Teaching a doctrine is rather meaningless.** I am not a philosopher; my mind is anti-philosophical because philosophy has led nowhere and cannot lead. The mind which thinks and the mind which questions cannot know.

There are so many doctrines, and infinite possibilities for many more. But a doctrine is a fiction – a human fiction; not a discovery but an invention. The human mind is capable of creating so many systems and doctrines, but to know the truth through theories is an impossibility. And a mind stuffed with knowledge is a mind which is bound to remain ignorant.

Knowledge comes the moment knowledge ceases. The known must cease for the unknown to be. And the truth and the real is unknown. There are two possibilities: either you think about it, or we go into it existentially. Thinking is something around and around, about and about, but never the reality. One can go on thinking for ages. The more you think, the farther away you go. That which *is*, is here and now. And to think about it is to lose contact with it.

So what I am teaching – I am teaching an anti-doctrinaire, anti-philosophical, anti-speculative experience. How to be, just to *be*. How to be in the moment that is here and now. Open, vulnerable, one with it. That's what I call meditation.

*Osho,*
*Do you think it is possible to link knowledge, speculative knowledge, theory, or doctrine with experience? Is it possible to try both and not only one?*

**It is not possible** to try both because they are diametrically opposite dimensions. You cannot try both.

*Is it not possible to subordinate knowledge? To consider it as subordinate to experience, but not to exclude it as a possibility of the human mind?*

**It is a possibility,** it is a possibility of the human mind, but a possibility which leads into fiction.

*If it is dominating…*

**If it is at all! It leads into fiction.** It leads the mind into projecting things. It is a dream faculty, a faculty of the imagination. So both are not possible. But once you have known the real then you can use knowledge as a vehicle to express it – but not as a means of achieving it. Knowledge cannot be a vehicle toward the truth, but when the truth has been known it can be a vehicle. It can be a vehicle as a communicative medium.

Once you want to communicate, to share something with someone who has not known it, only then your knowledge, your words, your language, your doctrines and theories can become a means. But still not adequate. It is still a faltering means, a means which is bound to falsify – because something that has been known existentially cannot be expressed totally. You can just indicate, you can symbolize it. But the symbol goes – the symbol is communicated and the meaning is left behind. What I have known, the moment I express it, the word goes to you but the meaning is left behind – a word which is dead, in a way meaningless, only apparently meaningful, because the meaning was the experience.

So knowledge can become a vehicle of expression, but not a means toward the achievement, toward the realization. And both cannot go simultaneously. The knowing mind is a hindrance. The mind which thinks in terms of knowledge becomes a hindrance. It becomes a hindrance because when you know then you are not humble. When you are stuffed with knowledge then there is no space within you to receive the unknown. So the mind must become vacant, a void, a womb, a receptivity, a total receptivity without any knowledge in its possession, without the knowing attitude. As far as the truth, the existential truth, is concerned, you, you cannot survive with your knowledge now.

You must discard the accumulated knowledge because… There are so many things: first, knowledge is your past. It is what you have known. It is your memory, it is your accumulation, it is your possession. This accumulation must

## The Fallacy of Knowledge

become a barrier; it must come between you and the new which is coming to you. It has to be discarded. It must not be between you and the unknown.

You must be open to the unknown, and you can only be open when you are humble in your ignorance. So be aware of one's ignorance, be constantly aware, constantly aware that something is still unknown, and that knowledge must not come between me and the act, the unknown. But a mind which has based itself on memories, information, scriptures, theories, doctrines, dogmas is a mind which becomes egocentric, which is not humble. Knowledge cannot give you humbleness. Only the vast unknown makes you humble, makes you submissive to it, and makes you surrender yourself to it.

So the memory must cease. Not just that there should be no memory in between, but in the moment of knowing, in the moment of experiencing, the memory must not be there. In that moment a total, vulnerable mind is required. At this moment of emptiness is meditation, is *dhyana*.

*There are many points. How do you experience, how do you realize this void? What is the possibility of each individual to have this kind of experience, what you communicate to us by knowledge – doctrine of the antidoctrine, using knowledge as communication – and dangerously, as you put it. Behind the words expressing this truth of the "void mind," how do you realize this? Is it possible to explain it in words?*

**Knowledge can become a negative connotation.** Through words, through language and through symbols the positive experience cannot be communicated, but the negativity can be communicated. I cannot say what it is, but I can say what it is not. Language can become a vehicle as far as the negativity is concerned. When I say language cannot express it, I am still expressing it. When I say no doctrine is possible about it, I am still using a doctrine. But this is negative. I am simply denying. I am not saying something. I am not saying something, I am denying something. The "no" can be said; the "yes" cannot be. The "yes" has to be realized; the "no" can be said.

One thing, potentially…it is very personal to ask: how can this moment of void be achieved? That is the most important and significant question. This void can be achieved, obviously, through living. First, the futility of knowledge must be understood as a background. If there is a lingering belief in knowledge, that will become a hindrance in achieving the void. So the first thing to be understand is the futility of the past, of the known, of knowledge, of the mind which is crammed with memories – the futility of it. As far as the unknown is concerned, the true is concerned, it can be…it can be an awareness, an awareness of what the mind has known.

There are two possibilities.

Either you become identified with what you have known, or you become a witness to what you have known. If you become identified with it – not that you have known it but you have become the knowledge – you and your memory are one in identification. If the mind is identified, the consciousness is identified with the content of knowledge; then the void will become difficult. But if there is no identification, if you have remained aloof from your memories – memories are there as a part of your accumulation, but you are aloof, separate, not

## The Fallacy of Knowledge

identified with them – you are aware of yourself as something different from your memories. This awareness becomes a path toward the void.

The more you become aware, the more you become a witness of your knowledge. The less you are the knower, the less is the possibility of your ego becoming a possessor, a knower. If you are different from your memories...and one *is* different. Memories have come just like dust accumulating. They have come through experiences and have become a part and parcel of our mind, but still, the consciousness is different. The one who remembers is different from that which is remembered. The one who has known is different from that which has been known. If this distinction becomes clear and clarity is achieved, the void comes nearer and nearer. Unidentified, you can be open; you can be without memory coming between you and the unknown.

The void can be achieved, but this void cannot be created. If you create it, it is bound to be created by your old mind, your knowledge. So there can be no method because a method can only come from your accumulated information. And if there is any method to cultivate the void it is bound to be a continuity with your old mind. It will not be a discontinuous experience. And the new, the unknown, must come to you not as a continuity, but as a discontinuous gap. Only then is it beyond your knowledge.

So there can be no method as such, there can be no methodology; only the understanding, only the awareness that "I am separate from that which I have accumulated." If this is to be understood, then there is no need of any cultivation; but things will happen. I am unidentified so *I* am the void. Now there is no need to create it.

And one cannot create it because a created void will not be a void. It will be your creation and your creation can never be nothingness, void, or be emptiness. It cannot be this space which is unlimited – because my creation, your creation, will be a limited creation; something with boundaries. I have created it.

The void must come to me. I can only be a receiver, so I can only be prepared in a negative way – prepared in the sense that I am not identified with knowledge; prepared in the sense that I have understood the futility, the meaninglessness of what I have known.

Only this awareness of the thinking process can lead me and others – can lead me into a jump, into a gap where that which *is* overwhelms me, that which *is* always present comes to me and I go to it, and there is no barrier between me and it. Now it has become one infinite moment, one eternity, one infinity.

But the moment you have known it, again you will translate it into knowledge. Again it will become part and parcel of your memory, again it will be lost. So no one can ever say, "I have known." The unknown always remains. Whatsoever one may know from it, the unknown remains the same. The charm of it, the beauty of it, the attraction of it, the call of it, remains the same.

So the process of knowing is eternal. One can never come to a point where he can say, "I have reached." And if someone says this he has fallen into the pattern of memory, into the pattern of knowledge again, which becomes a death. The moment one asserts knowledge is the moment of his death. Life has ceased because life is always from the unknown toward the unknown. Always and always, beyond and beyond.

## The Fallacy of Knowledge

To know a religious person is not to know a person who claims knowledge. A person who claims knowledge may be a theologian, may be a philosopher, but not a religious mind. A religious mind accepts the ultimate mystery, the ultimate unknowableness, the ultimate ecstasy of ignorance, the ultimate bliss of it.

This moment cannot be created, it cannot be projected. If you cannot make your mind still, if you *make* it, either you have intoxicated it or you have hypnotized it. But this is not the void, the void which comes and can never be brought.

So I am not teaching any method in the sense that there are methods, techniques, doctrines. I am not a teacher.

*First of all, you speak of a negative preparation, the philosophy of knowledge and the distance you should have from it, turning toward your true seeker – the true as opposed to the false one; you point out the true seeker. So when you're talking about the philosophy of knowledge which indirectly is linked with the death of knowledge, what I think is the main problem for most of us is that we already know the words, we know the verses, we are aware of the danger of knowledge intellectually. Intellectually we might be aware of the danger of knowledge but it is still on an intellectual level.*
*How to transform the "right" knowledge? You are saying, and I can agree with you, that knowledge is dangerous, but how can you transform a conviction?*
*I might see somewhere that you are right, but how to transform my conviction to the kind of intuitive knowledge*

*or "void," as you use the word? How to transform these convictions to the intuitive grasping of the truth? How to relate to the void?*

**If you are convinced** then there is no need of any transformation. But we are not convinced and we cannot be. We cannot be – how can one be convinced?

One can know and be convinced, but not through somebody else, not through me. How can you be convinced? And if you are convinced, this conviction's existence is bound to be intellectual. But an intellectual conviction is no conviction at all!

I am not trying to convince you. I am just conveying to you, I am just conveying to you a fact. I am not trying to convince you.

*What is the link between conviction and experience? Because I agree with you that you are not convinced if you are not already talking of something you have experienced. How to transform this to the kind of truth so I can say, "This is true"?*

**I understand.** There is no "how," because "how" means some method. There is an awakening; there is no "how." If you are listening to me and something is felt by you, that "this might be true"... If this happens to you, "This feeling, this means this might be true"... Why does this happen to you? Because, there are two things: either you are convinced by my argument, or you see it as a fact in yourself. These are two things.

## The Fallacy of Knowledge

If my argument becomes a conviction then you will ask "how?" If what I am saying is experienced by you as a fact, that "Yes, knowledge is something apart from me. I am not the knowledge." If this happens as an experience while I am talking, there is a possibility of it happening. There is also a possibility of my argument going into your mind. If my argument goes there, then there will be a question of "how."

When the intellect is convinced, it asks "how? – what is the method to know it?" But I am not giving you any argument. I am not giving you any doctrine. I am just telling you of my experience. And I know all the while that both these possibilities are there.

When you are listening you may listen to it as someone saying something to you, or you may listen to it as something happening within you. When I say memory is something accumulated apart from me, that memory is something dead, a hangover of the past, that which I have known, that it is something from the past hanging with me, but I am separate… When I am talking about this, if this happens to you as a feeling, and if you come to a glimpse about your process of memory, and about you, and the distance between the two – the process of memory and your consciousness – then there is no "how." Then something has happened, and this something can go on penetrating, not through any method, but through your awareness, day to day, moment to moment – about your knowledge, about your memory and about your self – this remembrance, this constant remembrance, around something different from what I have *known*.

Consciousness is something different from the content of consciousness. If this becomes an awareness moment to moment – when you are walking, when you are talking, when you are seeing, when you are eating, when you are going to sleep – if this becomes a constant awareness: that I am something apart from the memory that is being cultivated, accumulated, that is being built in in the mind, this mind is a computer, a computerized, built-in process… If this becomes an awareness, not a method, if you become aware of it, then something will happen.

No one can say when, no one can say how, no one can say where. If this awareness goes on, goes on, goes on, it goes deeper and deeper by itself. This is an automatic process. It becomes deeper: from the intellect it goes to your heart; and from the intelligence it goes to your intuitive mind; from the conscious slowly and slowly it goes into the unconscious. Someday you are totally awakened. Something has happened – not as a cultivation, but as a by-product of your remembering of a fact. Not by any cultivation of any fiction, doctrine, principle, technique, but as an awakening to an inner fact, inner division, something has gone deep in you.

When the moment comes, it comes completely unpredicted, unknown, as an explosion. And in that moment of explosion, you are completely empty – you are not. You have ceased to be. There is no intellect, there is no reason, there is no memory. There is simple consciousness: consciousness of the void. And in that void is the realization, in that void is the achievement, in that void is the knowledge, but knowledge in quite another sense. Now there is no knower; now there is no known. There is simple flowing knowing; only the knowing exists. This is existential.

And this cannot be communicated. What exists in that

## The Fallacy of Knowledge

void, what that void is cannot be communicated. But all except that can be communicated. Obviously it will be negative because the innermost, the real-most, the ultimate, is not communicated – only the passage, the process. And that process cannot be conceived as a method because a method is to be practiced. Remembrance cannot be practiced. Either you remember, or you don't.

*Experience through awareness, if I understand. When you classify negatively, or, don't define, but indicate negatively, what might be the result arrived at from discarding thoughts from true experience? You mention yoga sometimes... Do you recommend or do you practice these kind of exercises, or is it exclusively a kind of inner soul search? Do you think a special kind of life or a special way of living is necessary to achieve or to progress?*

**No. No special living is required,** but the moment you become aware, your living changes, your life will change. But those changes will come to you; they will not be practiced. The moment you practice something, it loses whatsoever is significant in it. It must come to you as a spontaneity.

*But how to be with spontaneity because you might wish to be aware of the awareness?*

**No, don't wish.** There is no question of wishing. Don't wish. Just be; don't wish.

*The Psychology of the Esoteric*

> *No…because to wish is contrary to what you are saying, That would be contradictory in terms, to give any such advice – that if you want the void, don't wish for the it. So I quite agree with you. But is it just to realize little by little and find the void, not realizing by wishing or wanting, or doing something?*
> *I understand this, but how to stop the wish?*

**No, no, no.** There is no question of stopping the wish. There is only the question of understanding. There is no question of anything being stopped or anything being practiced. The question is simply to understand that you cannot long for the void. It is not only a contradiction in terms; it is a contradiction existentially too. If it was only a contradiction in terms then there would be every possibility that it may not be so serious, but if it is existentially contradictory…

You cannot wish because the wish comes somehow from the "old mind," somehow "knowledge" – the wish comes from *you*. And you must not be there. So you cannot wish; you can only understand. And by understanding you cease to be. You can simply understand that this is the fact: that I cannot wish for it, I cannot long for it, I cannot desire it. All that I can do is to be aware of what I am.

If I become aware of what I am, then I become aware of two things. One: that I have been thinking I am but I am not. And two: that I have never known. When I become aware of me as I am in this moment, there happens to be a separation, a division, a partition. Something of me becomes unidentified with something of me.

Then there are two: I and me. The "me" is the memory, the "me" is the mind; and the "I" is the consciousness, the

## The Fallacy of Knowledge

"I" is the *atman*. So I am not to do anything; I am to be aware of what I am in this very moment. Simply aware without any method.

Someone may come to you and he may put a dagger to your chest. In this moment – for a single fraction of moment – you become aware of just what *is*. There is no method. You don't ask them "How am I to be aware of it?" You just become aware of the situation. And in that moment there is no meditation. In that moment there is no mind. In that moment there is no "me." In that moment the "I" is and the dagger is, and the situation, and there is nothing between. But that moment exists for a fraction of a second – the "me" comes in and begins to work: "What to do?"

From moments of danger, sometimes spontaneously you become aware. There is every possibility that because of this, there will be a hankering for danger. Then the danger is asked for, is sought, because of that moment, that fragment of a moment, that awareness.

If you are listening to me and are not thinking in terms of what to do about it afterward, but are simply listening to me, after some time you become aware. And don't ask how because that is an impossibility. Become aware of what I am saying as an inner process – then you see it, then it becomes a conviction, not through my argument but through *your* remembering of a fact.

Simultaneously you must listen to me and listen to your inner mind, of the process going on inside all the time. What I say is becoming a part of your "me," it is becoming part of your me – it is becoming part of your knowledge. This knowledge will ask how to transform; this knowledge will ask for further knowledge – about the "how," about the method. And if some method is shown, that too will become part of your knowledge. Your "me" will be strengthened, will become more knowledgeable.

My emphasis is not about your "me." I am not talking with your "me." If your "me" comes in then the communication cannot become a communion. It is simply a communication – a discussion, not a dialogue. It becomes a dialogue if there is no "me." If you are there – no, if you are *here* not through your "me," then there is no question of "how." What I am saying is that it will either be seen as a truth or as an untruth, either as a fact or as hocus-pocus doctrinaire. If it is a fact then something has happened; if it is a fiction then there is no question.

So I am concerned to create a situation either by talking, or by silence, or by teaching you in a way to create a situation, where your "I" comes in a form of…your "I" comes out, your "I" goes beyond your "me." So what I am doing with my friends is just trying to create many situations.

*What kind of situations?*

**This too is a kind of situation,** this too is a kind of situation. I am saying absurd things to you, absurd! Because I am saying to achieve something, and still denying any method. This is absurd! Now I am saying something and still saying that it cannot be said, which is absurd.

*But it is the only possible way.*

## The Fallacy of Knowledge

**It is the only possible way!** It is the only possible way because it is the absurdity in itself that can create the situation. If I am convincing to you then it will not create the situation. It will become part of your "me," of your knowledge. No. I must be convincing in a way that your "me" is not convinced. Your "me" goes on asking: "How? What is the way?" I will deny the way and still talk of the transformation. Only then does the situation become absurd, the situation become so irrational that your mind is not satisfied. Then something from beyond can take over, can take over the meaning.

So I am creating situations, all the time I am creating situations. As I know an intellectual person, so absurdity must be the situation for an intellectual. A person who…

*An intellectual person and the absurd: this is a contradiction.*

**No, that is the potential,** that is the potential; that has to be appealed to, that *has* to be appealed to.

With a non-intellectual person, absurdity has no meaning. Something else will appeal to him. So it differs from individual to individual. When a person comes to me, it means that if I love him he is put into an absurd situation, so that he becomes aware. We become aware only when something absurd has happened, something that cannot be put into the continuity – something that is bound to create a gap, something shattering, disturbing. So that this disturbance – a disturbance which is a disturbance to you may not be a disturbance to me, or to someone else.

I am reminded of an anecdote of Buddha.

*The Psychology of the Esoteric*

One morning someone asks him, "Is there a God? I believe, I am a believer, and I believe in the supreme God"

Buddha denied it absolutely. "There is no God. There has never been one and there is no possibility. What absurd nonsense are you saying!" The man is shattered, but the situation has been created.

In the afternoon, another man comes to Buddha and says, "I am atheist; I don't believe in any God. Is there any God? What do you say?"

Buddha says, "Only God is. Nothing else exists except him." The man is shattered.

But a monk who is always accompanying Buddha is shattered much more because he had heard both the answers. He finds a time when Buddha is alone so that "I may be put at ease." The monk is in anguish: in the morning Buddha has said, "There is no God"; in the afternoon, "Only God is." In the evening a third man comes and asks the Buddha, "I am an agnostic. I neither believe nor disbelieve. What do you think? Is there a God or is there not?" Buddha remained silent. The man is shattered – but the monk all the more.

That night the monk, Ananda, asks Buddha, "Please Buddha, first answer me. You have taken my ultimate truth. I am at a loss! What do you mean by these absurd answers, contradictory answers?"

Buddha says, "Neither answer was given to you. Why have you taken them? Those answers were given to the persons who were asking. Why have you listened?"

The man said, "You are putting me into still more absurdity. I was with you so I have heard them both, but they are disturbing."

## The Fallacy of Knowledge

Buddha said, "So now I will go to sleep. Remain in your disturbance."

A situation can be created. There is this possibility: a situation can be created. A Zen monk creates one in his own way. He may push you out of a door, or slap you on your face, and a situation is created which is absurd. You had asked something; he will answer something else. Someone asks, "What is the way?" and a Zen monk answers – is not concerned at all with the way – he says, "See that river." or "See that tree. How tall it is!" or "See the leaves, how they filter." This is absurd.

The mind seeks continuum. It is afraid of absurdity. It is afraid of the irrational, and the unknown is beyond him. It is erratic. And the truth is not a by-product of intellectualization. The truth is neither a deduction or an induction. It is not logic. It is not a conclusion.

So I can simply say I am creating a situation. I am not conveying anything to you. I am just creating a situation, and if the situation is created, something which is unconveyable can be conveyed.

So don't ask "how." Just be. Be aware if you can. If you cannot, be aware of your "cannot." Be aware; if you cannot be aware, be aware of your unawareness. Be attentive to what is. If you cannot be, be attentive of your inattention. And the thing will happen. The thing happens.

*When you see it happening, how do you expect the experience to be? Is it possible that the feeling created is not a good space; it is already so totally absurd as you have said. This possibility of disturbing other people – is it a risk?*

**No. No. People are disturbed already.** But because they are disturbed already, they have become identified with the disturbance. They have become at ease with it. It has become habitual. It has become everything. We are disturbed already – because how is it possible that a person can be undisturbed and not know the truth?

Disturbance is our situation. When I disturb you, your disturbance is disturbed. So quite the contrary appears. Disturbance disturbed is negative. You become for the first time calm. The reason is disturbance is not there now. This is not the result; rather this is the way to convey a message which is essentially unconveyable.

What you are asking, you are asking, "What will be achieved? What will be the result?" Something can be said, with the condition that it should not be taken as truth. It should only be taken as symbolic, as poetic, as a myth. If you take it as a myth it is possible that a thing may be indicated. If you take it as the truth there is every possibility that the thing may be hindering.

With the myth, the thing is that every scripture that is religious is a myth, and every assertion that comes from a person who has gone through the happening, is in a sense untrue – until you understand that it can only indicate. It is not the truth, but only an indicator. And the indicator must be forgotten before the truth can be known.

There are three words which are the last line, the boundary line; beyond that comes silence. These boundary words are *sat-chit-anand*, *sat-chit-anand*: existence – pure existence; bliss – pure bliss; consciousness – pure consciousness. These three are words that create as one. These three words are phases of it, or not even phases. When we make a concept of

## The Fallacy of Knowledge

it, it becomes divided into three. It is experienced as one, but conceptualized as three.

These three: total existence, absolute existence, authentic is-ness, authenticity of is-ness. You are, only you are. Neither this nor that. Simply is-ness – you are not this nor that. You *are*; being, unidentified with anything. That's why it is "pure."

Second: bliss. Not happiness, not joy: bliss. Happiness has a shade of unhappiness, a remembrance, a contrast. Joy, too, has tensions overflowing, not at ease, continual tension, which is bound to be released to go down. But bliss, bliss is happiness without any shade of unhappiness. Bliss is joy without any abyss around it, going downwards. Bliss is non-dual happiness – the true joy. There is no contradictory term for bliss. It is the midpoint.

The contradictory terms are always of the extremes – of one extreme or of the other. Joy is one, sorrow the other. Bliss is the midpoint or the beyond point or the transcendent. It has both the depth of sorrow and the height of joy. Joy is never deep. It is superfluous. It has a height, no depth. Sorrow is deep, it has a depth – an abysmal depth, but no peak. Bliss is both: the light of the joy and the darkness of sorrow; depth and height both, simultaneously. So it transcends both. The light is pure. Only a non-extreme midpoint can be a point of transcendence.

And the third is consciousness, *chit*. *Chit* is not our conscious mind, because our conscious mind is a fragment of a greater unconscious one. It is not the consciousness which has with it the unconscious. When you are conscious you are conscious of something. Our consciousness is always objective; it is about something. *Chit* consciousness is simply consciousness, about nothing. It is conscious and conscious not of any object; a light. But we never see light. We see only lightened objects. We never see the light; light is never seen – only the object with the light. A light-fallen object is seen; light as such is never seen. So we never know consciousness, we know a consciousness which is always objective of something. *Chit* is absolute consciousness, consciousness as light, not as the lighted object. Consciousness not arrowed against something, but unarrowed. That light can be infinite and pure. There is no object in it. Nothing can make it impure. It is and it is and it is.

These three terms, *sat-chit-anand*, these terms are positive. So these are the boundary terms, at the most what can be said. But this is the least of what can be experienced. This is the last boundary of expression and the first jump into the unexpressed. From here – not that here is the end. From here is the beginning, from this point our mind can have a glimpse. This glimpse, too, is of our world, of our knowledge, of our minds.

So this is the expression, not the real. If this is remembered, then no harm is done. But our mind forgets it, and this expression *sat-chit-anand* becomes a reality. So we go around these theories, doctrines, and the mind becomes closed. Then there is no jump. This misfortune has happened in India. In this land the whole tradition has been woven around these three words – around the Upanishads, the Vedanta, the Sankhya, all around these three words. And these are boundary words, the frontier of the mind. So the reality is not *sat-chit-anand*; it is beyond, but with a "how much can be put into words," it should be taken as a parable. The whole of religious literature is a parable; something said and done in words – verbalized – which is intrinsically inexpressible.

## The Fallacy of Knowledge

I always fear to even use these words as myths, because the moment the mind knows what will happen there, it begins to create theses, it begins to long for it. It begins to ask and demand and desire. When it demands *sat-chit-anand*, when it demands *sat-chit-anand* then there are teachers who supply the demand. It demands methods, demands mantra, tantra, technique, method; and there are teachers. Every demand will be supplied. The nonsensical demand will be supplied by nonsense; an absurd demand is supplied by absurdity. All theologies and all gurudoms are created in this way.

So one has to be aware all the time not to make the ultimate into a desired whim; not to make it a wish, an object; not to make it something somewhere far off, to be achieved and to be traveled to. It is just here and now. And if we can become aware of other inner processes, the explosion can happen. It is already around, it is our nearmost neighbor, but we go on, far off. It is right beside us, and we go on a long pilgrimage. It always follows us like a shadow, but we never see it because our eyes are far off, are eyes are *far* off. We are always hankering for the distant.

If one becomes a becoming and loses the desire, life must become being in the present. There is a saying of Lao Tzu: "Seek, and you will lose. Do not seek, and find." The man who seeks goes far off. The man who is, and is not seeking realizes the near one. Even to say the "near one" is absurd because the near one, too, is distant. It is "I," not even the neighbor, but the owner of the house. The neighbor, too, is distant. It is the host. And the host has gone out.

# 10/ *Truth, Goodness, Beauty: Windows to the Divine*

*Osho,*
*In Indian philosophy, the nature of ultimate truth has been described as truth, satyam, beauty, sundaram and goodness, shivam. Are these the characteristics of godliness?*

**These are not the qualities of godliness.** Rather, they are our experiences of it. They do not belong to the divine as such; they are our perceptions. The divine, by itself, is unknowable. Either it is every quality, or no quality at all. But as the human mind is constituted, it can experience the divine through three windows: you can have the glimpse either through beauty or through truth or through goodness. These three dimensions belong to the human mind. They are our limitations. The frame is given by us; the divine itself is frameless.

It is like this. We can see the sky through the

## Truth, Goodness, Beauty: Windows to the Divine

window. The window looks like a frame around the sky, but the sky itself has no frame around it. It is infinite. Only the window gives it a frame. In the same way, beauty, truth and goodness are the windows through which we can glance into the divine.

Human personality is divided into three layers. If intellect is predominant, then the divine takes the shape of truth. The intellectual approach creates the window of truth, the frame of truth. If the mind is emotional, if one comes to reality not through the head but through the heart, then the divine becomes beauty. The poetic quality is given by you. It is only the frame. Intellect gives it the frame of truth; emotion gives it the frame of beauty. And if the personality is neither emotional nor intellectual – if action is predominant – then the frame becomes goodness.

So here in India we use these three terms for the divine. Bhakti yoga means the way of devotion and is for the emotional type. Godliness is seen as beauty. Gyan yoga is the way of knowledge. Godliness is seen as truth. And karma yoga is the way of action. Godliness is goodness.

The very word *god* comes from the word *good*. This word has had the greatest influence because most of humanity is predominantly active, not intellectual or emotional. This does not mean that there is no intellect or emotion, but they are not predominant factors. Very few are intellectual and very few are emotional. The majority of humanity is predominantly active. Through action, God becomes "the good."

But the opposite pole must exist too, so if God is perceived as the good then the Devil will be perceived as the bad. The active mind will perceive the Devil as the bad; the emotional mind will perceive the Devil as the ugly; and

*The Psychology of the Esoteric*

the intellectual mind will perceive the Devil as the untrue, the illusory, the false.

These three characteristics — truth, goodness and beauty — are human categories framed around the divine, which is in itself frameless. They are not qualities of the divine as such. If the human mind can perceive the divine through any fourth dimension, then this fourth dimension will also become a quality of the divine. I don't mean that the divine is not the good. I'm only saying that this goodness is a quality that is chosen by us and seen by us. If man did not exist in the world then the divine would not be good, the divine would not be beautiful, the divine would not be true. Divinity would exist all the same, but these qualities, which are chosen by us, would not be there. These are just human perceptions. We can perceive the divine to be other qualities as well.

We do not know if animals perceive the divine. We do not know how they perceive things at all, but one thing is certain: they will not perceive the divine in human terms. If they perceive the divine at all, they will feel and perceive it in quite a different way from us. The qualities they perceive will not be the same as they are for us.

When a person is predominantly intellectual, he cannot conceive of how you can say godliness is beautiful. The very concept is absolutely foreign to his mind. And a poet cannot conceive that truth can mean anything except beauty. It cannot mean anything else to him. Truth is beauty; all else is simply intellectual. For a poet, for a painter, for a man who perceives the world in terms of the heart, truth is a naked thing without beauty. It is just an intellectual category.

So if a particular mind is predominantly intellectual, it

## Truth, Goodness, Beauty: Windows to the Divine

cannot understand the emotional mind, and vice versa. That is why there is so much misunderstanding and so many definitions. No single definition can be accepted by the whole of humanity. Godliness must come to you in your own terms. When you define godliness, you will be part of the definition. The definition will come from you; it as such is indefinable. So those who look at it through these three windows have, in a way, imposed themselves, their own definitions, on the divine.

There is also the possibility of a fourth way of seeing the divine for one who has transcended these three dimensions in his personality. In India, we do not have a word for the fourth. We simply call it *turiya*, the fourth. There is a type of consciousness where you are neither intellectual nor emotional nor active, but just conscious. Then you are not looking at the sky through any window. You have come out of your house and you know the windowless sky. There is no pattern, no frame.

Only the type of consciousness that has realized the fourth can understand the limitations of the other three. It can understand the difficulty of understanding among the others, and can also understand the underlying similarities among beauty, truth and goodness. Only the fourth type can understand and tolerate. The other three types will always be quarreling.

All religions belong to one of these three categories. And they have been constantly quarreling. Buddha cannot take part in this conflict. He belongs to the fourth type. He says, "It is all nonsense. You are not quarreling about divine qualities; you are quarreling about your windows. The sky remains the same from any window."

So these are not divine qualities. These are divine qualities as perceived by us. If we can destroy our windows, we can know the divine as quality-less, *nirgun*. Then we go beyond qualities. Only then does human projection not come in.

But then it becomes very difficult to say anything. Whatever can be said about the divine can be said only through the windows, because anything that can be said is really being said about the windows, not about the sky itself. When we see beyond the windows, the sky is so vast, so limitless. It cannot be defined. All words are inapplicable; all theories are inadequate.

So one who is in the fourth has always remained silent about it, and definitions of the divine have come from the first three. If the one in the fourth has spoken at all, he has spoken in terms that seem absurd, illogical, irrational. He contradicts himself. Through contradiction he tries to show something. Not to say something; to show something.

Wittgenstein has made this distinction. He said that there are truths that can be said, and there are truths that can be shown but not said. A thing is definable because it exists among other things. It can be related to other things, compared. For example, we can always say that a table is not a chair. We can define it by reference to something else. It has a boundary to which it extends, and beyond which something else begins. Really, only the boundary is defined. A definition means the boundary from which everything else begins.

But we cannot say anything about the divine. The divine is the total, so there is no boundary; there is no frontier from which something else begins. There is no "something else." The divine is frontierless so it cannot be defined.

## Truth, Goodness, Beauty: Windows to the Divine

The fourth can only show; it can only indicate. That is why the fourth has remained mysterious. And the fourth is the most authentic, because it is not colored by human perceptions. All the great saints have indicated; they have not said anything. Whether it is Jesus, Buddha, Mahavira or Krishna, it doesn't matter. They are not saying anything; they are just indicating something – just a finger pointing to the moon.

But there is always the difficulty that you will become obsessed by the finger. The finger is meaningless; it is indicating something else. It must not catch your eye. If you want to see the moon, the finger must be absolutely forgotten.

This has been the greatest difficulty as far as the divine is concerned. You see the indication and you feel that this indication is, itself, the truth. Then the whole purpose is destroyed. The finger is not the moon; they are absolutely different. The moon can be shown by the finger, but one must not cling to the finger. If a Christian cannot forget the Bible, if a Hindu cannot forget the Gita, then the very purpose is destroyed. The whole thing becomes purposeless, meaningless and in a way non-religious, anti-religious.

Whenever one approaches the divine, one must be aware of one's own mind. If one approaches the divine through the mind, the divine becomes colored by it. If you approach the divine without mind, without you, without the human coming in, if you approach the divine as an emptiness, as a void, a nothingness, without any preconceptions, without any propensity for seeing things in a particular way – then you know the quality-lessness of the divine, otherwise not. Otherwise all the qualities we give to the divine belong to our human windows. We impose them upon the divine.

*Are you saying that we do not need to use the window to see the sky?*

**Yes. It is better to look from the window** than not to look at all, but to look through the window cannot be compared to the windowless sky.

*But how does one get from the room to the sky without the window?*

**You can pass through the window** to go to the sky, but you must not remain at the window. Otherwise the window will always be there. The window must be left behind. It must be passed through and transcended.

*Once one is in the sky there are no words – until one comes back into the room. Then the story comes…*

**Yes, one can come back.** But then he cannot be the same as he was before. He has known the patternless, the infinite. Then even from the window he knows that the sky is not patterned, not windowed. Even from behind the window he cannot be deceived. Even if the window is closed and the room becomes dark, he knows that the infinite sky is there. Now he cannot be the same again.

Once you have known the infinite, you have become the infinite. We are what we have known, what we have felt. Once you have known the boundless, the boundary-less, in a way you have become infinite. To know something is to be that. To know love is to be love; to know prayerfulness is to be prayerfulness; to know the divine is to be the divine. Knowing is realization; knowing is being.

*Do all three windows become one?*

**No. Each window will remain as it was.** The window has not changed; you have changed. If the person is emotional he will go out and come in through that window, but now he will not deny other windows; he will not be antagonistic to them. Now he will be understanding of the others. He will know that other windows also lead to the same sky.

Once you have been under the sky, you know that the other windows are part of the same house. Now you may wander to other windows or you may not. It depends on you. You need not; one window is enough. If a person is like Ramakrishna he may wander to other windows to see whether the same sky is seen through them. It depends on the person. One may look through other windows or one may not.

And really, there is no need. To know the sky is enough. But one may inquire, be curious. Then he will look through other windows. There have been persons who have wandered and persons who have not. But once a person has known the open sky, he will not deny other windows; he will not deny other approaches. He will confirm that their windows open to the same thing. So a person who has known the sky becomes religious, not sectarian. The sectarian mind remains behind the window; the religious mind is beyond it.

One who has seen the sky may wander; he may go to other windows also. There are infinite windows. These are the main types, but they are not the only windows. There are so many combinations possible.

*Is there a window for every consciousness, for each man?*

**Yes. In a way each person comes to the divine** from his own window. And each window is basically different from any other. Infinite are the windows, infinite are the sects. Each person has a sect of his own. Two Christians are not the same. One Christian differs from another as much as Christianity differs from Hinduism.

Once you have come to the sky, you know that all differences belong to the house. They never belong to you. They belong to the house in which you lived, through which you saw, through which you felt, but not to you as such.

When you come under the sky, you know that you were also part of the sky – only living within walls. The sky within the house is not different from the sky beyond the house. Once we come out we know that the barriers were not real. Even a wall is not a barrier to the sky; it has not divided the sky at all. It creates an appearance that the sky is divided – that this is my house and that house is yours; that the sky in my house belongs to me and the sky in your house belongs to you – but once you have come to know the sky itself, there is no difference. Then there are no individuals as such. Then waves are lost and only the ocean remains. You will come back inside again, but now you will not be different from the sky.

## Truth, Goodness, Beauty: Windows to the Divine

*It seems there are so few Christians who have gone to the sky and who have come back with this concept.*

**There are some** – Saint Francis, Eckhart, Boehme…

*They didn't tell us it was the same sky, did they?*

**They could not.** The sky is always the same, but they cannot report on the sky in the same way. Reports about the sky are bound to be different, but what is being reported is not different. To those who have not known the reported thing itself, the report will be everything. Then the differences become acute. But all that is reported is just a selection, a choice. The whole cannot be reported; only a part of the whole can be reported. And when it is reported, it becomes dead.

Saint Francis can report only as a Saint Francis can report. He cannot report like Mohammed, because the report does not come from the sky. The report comes from the pattern, from the individuality. It comes from the mind: the memory, the education, the experiences; from the words, the language, the sect; from the living. The report comes from all that. It is not possible for the communication to come only from Saint Francis, because a report can never be individual. It must be communal or it will be an absolute failure.

If I report in my own individual language, no one will understand it. When I experienced the sky, I experienced it without the community. I was totally alone at the moment of knowing. There was no language; there were no words. But when I report, I report to others who have not known.

I must speak in their language. I will have to use a language that was known to me prior to my knowing.

Saint Francis uses the Christian language. As far as I am concerned, religions are only different languages. To me, Christianity is a particular language derived from Jesus Christ. Hinduism is another language; Buddhism is another language. The difference is always of language. But if one knows only the language and not the experience itself, the difference is bound to be vast.

Jesus said "the kingdom of God" because he was speaking in terms that could be understood by his audience. The word *kingdom* was understood by some and misunderstood by others. The cross followed, crucifixion followed. Those who understood Jesus understood what was meant by "the kingdom of God," but those who could not understand thought that he was dealing with a kingdom on earth.

But Jesus could not use Buddha's words. Buddha would never have used the word *kingdom*. There are so many reasons for the difference. Jesus came from a poor family; his language was that of a poor man. To a poor man the word *kingdom* is very expressive, but to Buddha there was nothing significant about the word because Buddha himself had been a prince. The word was meaningless for Buddha, but meaningful for Jesus.

Buddha became a beggar and Jesus became a king. That is bound to be. The other pole becomes meaningful. The unknown pole becomes expressive of the unknown. For Buddha, begging was the most unknown thing, so he took the form of the unknown, the form of a beggar. For him, *bhikkhu*, beggar, became the most significant term.

The word *bhikkhu* is never used in India because there

## Truth, Goodness, Beauty: Windows to the Divine

are so many beggars here. Instead, we use the word *swami*, master. When someone becomes a sannyasin, when he renounces, he becomes a swami, a master. But when Buddha renounced he became a *bhikkhu*, a beggar. For Buddha, this word carried something that it could not carry for Jesus.

Jesus could only speak in terms that were borrowed from Jewish culture. He could change something here and there, but he could not change the total language or no one would have been able to understand. So in a sense, he was not a Christian. By the time Saint Francis came along, a Christian culture had developed with its own language. So Saint Francis was more of a Christian than Christ himself. Christ remained a Jew; his whole life was Jewish. It could not be otherwise.

If you are born a Christian, then Christianity may not be expressive to you; it may not touch you. The more you have known it, the more it becomes meaningless. The mystery is lost. To a Christian, the Hindu attitude may be more meaningful, more significant. Because it is unknown, it can be expressive of the unknowable.

As far as I am concerned, it is better that a person not remain with the religion of his birth. The attitudes and beliefs that were given to him at birth must be denied sometime or the adventure will never begin. One should not remain where one was born. One should go to unknown corners and feel the exhilaration of it.

Sometimes we cannot understand the very thing that we think we have understood the most. A Christian thinks that he understands Christianity. That becomes the barrier. A Buddhist thinks he understands Buddhism because he knows it, but this very sense of knowing becomes a hindrance. Only the unknown can become the magnetic, the occult, the esoteric.

One must transcend the circumstances of one's birth. It is just circumstantial that one is a Christian by birth; it is just circumstantial that one is a Hindu by birth. One should not be confined to the conditions of his birth. One must be twice-born as far as religion is concerned. One must go to the unknown corners. Then the thrill is there; the exploration begins.

Religions are, in a way, complementary. They must work for others; they must accept others. A Christian or a Hindu or a Jew must know the thrill of conversion. The thrill of conversion creates the background for transformation. Whenever someone comes from the West to the East there is something new. The Eastern attitude is so different that it cannot be put into familiar categories. The whole attitude is so opposite to what you are familiar with that if you want to understand it, you yourself will have to change.

The same thing happens to someone from the East when he goes to the West – it should happen. One should be open so it can happen. It is the unknown, the unfamiliar, that will create a change.

In India, we could not create a religion like Christianity. We could not create a theology. We could not create the Vatican, the Church; there are temples, but there is no Church. The Eastern mind is basically illogical so it is bound to be chaotic in a sense. It is bound to be individual; it cannot be organizational.

A Catholic priest is something very different. He is trained to be part of an organization. He belongs somewhere in the hierarchy. And it works. An establishment, a hierarchy is logical, so Christianity has been able to be spread throughout the world.

Hinduism has never tried to convert anybody. Even if someone has converted himself, Hinduism is not at ease with him. It is a non-converting religion, non-organizational. There is no priesthood in the sense that exists in Catholicism. The Hindu monk is just a wandering individual – without any hierarchy, without belonging to any establishment. He is absolutely rootless. As far as the outside world is concerned this approach is bound to be a failure, but as far as the individual is concerned, as far as the inner depth is concerned, it is bound to be a success.

Vivekananda was very attracted to Christianity. He created the Order of Ramakrishna based on the pattern of the Catholic priesthood. This is very alien to the East, very foreign. It is absolutely Western. Vivekananda's mind was not Eastern at all. And just as I say that Vivekananda was Western, I say that Eckhart and Saint Francis were Eastern. Basically, they belonged to the East.

Jesus himself belonged to the East. But Christianity does not belong to the East; it belongs to the West. Jesus was basically Eastern; he was anti-church, anti-organization. That was the conflict.

The Western mind thinks in terms of logic, reason, system, argument. It cannot go very deep; it will remain on the surface. It will be extensive, but never intensive.

*So organized religions are a curtain to us. They will have to go in order for us to see the sky.*

**Yes. They cover the window,** they are obstacles.

*The Psychology of the Esoteric*

*Will the Western mind have to expand as the Eastern mind has?*

**The Western mind can succeed** as far as science is concerned, but it cannot succeed in religious consciousness. Whenever a religious mind is born, even in the West, it is Eastern. In Eckhart, in Boehme, the very quality of the mind is Eastern. And whenever a scientific mind is born in the East, it is bound to be Western. East and West are not geographical. West means the Aristotelian, and East means the non-Aristotelian. West means equilibrium, and East means no equilibrium. West means the rational and East means the irrational.

Tertullian was one of the most Eastern minds in the West. He said, "I believe in God because it is impossible to believe. I believe in God because it is absurd." This is the basic Eastern attitude: because it is absurd. No one can say this in the West. In the West they say that you should believe something only when it is rational. Otherwise it is just a belief, a superstition.

Eckhart, too, is an Eastern mind. He says, "If you believe in the possible, it is not a belief. If you believe in the argument, it is not religion. These are parts of science. Only if you believe in the absurd does something that is beyond mind come to you." This concept is not Western. It belongs to the East.

Confucius, on the other hand, is a Western mind. Those in the West can understand Confucius, but they can never understand Lao Tzu. Lao Tzu says, "You are a fool because you are only rational. To be rational, reasonable, is not enough. The irrational must have its own corner to exist. Only if a person is both rational and irrational is he reasonable."

A totally rational person can never be reasonable. Reason has its own dark corner of irrationality. A child is born in a

## Truth, Goodness, Beauty: Windows to the Divine

dark womb. A flower is born in the dark, in the underground roots. The dark must not be denied; it is the base. It is the most significant, the most life-giving thing.

The Western mind has something to contribute to the world; it is science, not religion. The Eastern mind can contribute only religion, not technology or science. Science and religion are complementary. If we can realize both their differences and their complementariness, then a better world culture can be born out of it.

If one needs science, one should go to the West. But if the West creates any religion, it can never be more than theology. In the West you give arguments to yourself to prove God. Arguments to prove God! It is inconceivable in the East. You cannot prove godliness. The very effort is meaningless. That which can be proven will never be it, it will be a scientific conclusion. In the East we say that the divine is the unprovable. When you are bored with your proofs, then jump into the experience itself; jump into the divine itself.

The Eastern mind can only be pseudo-scientific, just as the Western mind can only be pseudo-religious. You have created a great theology in the West, not a religious tradition. In the same way, whenever we make an attempt toward science in the East, we only create technicians not scientists, persons of know-how, not innovators, creators.

So do not come to the East with a Western mind or you will only misunderstand. Then you will carry your misunderstanding as an understanding. The attitude in the East is categorically opposite. Only opposites are complementary – like male and female.

The Eastern mind is female; the Western mind is male. The Western mind is aggressive. Logic is bound to be aggressive, violent. Religion is receptive, just like a woman. Godliness can only be received; it can never be discovered or invented. One has to become like a woman: totally receptive, just open and waiting. This is what is meant by meditation: to be open and waiting.

*Ramakrishna said that the bhakti approach is the most suitable for this age. Is that so?*

**No. Ramakrishna said** that bhakti yoga was the most suitable approach because it was the most suitable for him. That is the basic window through which he came under the sky. It is not a question of an approach being suitable or unsuitable for a particular age. We cannot think in terms of ages.

Centuries live contemporaneously – we seem to be contemporaries; we may not be. I may be living twenty centuries back. Nothing is absolutely past; for someone it is present. Nothing is absolutely future; for someone it is present. And nothing is absolutely present either. For someone it is past and for someone else it is yet to come. So no categorical statement can be made for the age as such.

Ramakrishna was a devotee. He came to godliness through prayerfulness and love, through emotion. He realized in this way, so for him it seemed that this would be helpful to everybody. He could not understand how his way might be difficult to others. However sympathetic we may be, we always see others in the light of our own experiences. So for Ramakrishna, the way seemed to be bhakti yoga: the way of devotion.

If we want to think in terms of ages, we can say that this age is the most intellectual, the most scientific, the most technological, the least devotional, the least emotional. What Ramakrishna was saying was right for him might have been right for the people who were with him, but Ramakrishna never affected the larger world. He belongs basically to the village, to the non-technological, non-scientific mind. He was a villager – uneducated, unacquainted with the greater world – so what he said should be understood according to his village language. He could not conceive of the days that have now come. He was basically part of the peasant's world where intellect was nothing and emotion was everything. He was not a man of this age. What he was saying was all right for the world in which he moved, but not for the world that exists now.

These three types have always existed: the intellectual, the active, the emotional. There will always be a balance among them, just as there is always a balance between males and females. The balance cannot be lost for long. If it is lost, it will soon be regained.

In the West you have lost the balance. Intellect has become the predominant factor. It may appeal to you that Ramakrishna says, "Devotion is the path for this age," because you have lost the balance. But Vivekananda says the opposite. Because the East has also lost the balance, he is predominantly intellectual. This is just to balance the existing extreme. It is complementary in a sense.

Ramakrishna was the emotional type and his chief disciple was the intellectual type. He was bound to be. That is the coupling: the male and the female. Ramakrishna is absolutely female: non-aggressive, receptive. Sex not only exists in biology; it exists everywhere. In every field, whenever there is polarity there is sex and the opposite becomes attracted.

Vivekananda could never be attracted to any intellectual. He could not be; he was not the polar opposite. There were intellectual giants in Bengal. He would go to visit them and would come away empty-handed. He would not be attracted. Ramakrishna was the least intellectual person possible. He was everything that Vivekananda was not, everything that he was seeking.

Vivekananda was the opposite of Ramakrishna, so what he taught in Ramakrishna's name was not in the same spirit as Ramakrishna's teaching itself. So whoever comes to Ramakrishna through Vivekananda can never come to Ramakrishna at all. Whoever understands Vivekananda's interpretation of Ramakrishna can never understand Ramakrishna himself. The interpretation comes from the polar opposite.

When people say, "Without Vivekananda we would never have known about Ramakrishna," it is right in a sense. The world at large would never have heard about Ramakrishna without Vivekananda. But with Vivekananda, whatever is known about Ramakrishna is basically false. It is a misinterpretation. This is because his type is quite contrary to Ramakrishna's type. Ramakrishna never argued; Vivekananda was argumentative. Ramakrishna was ignorant; Vivekananda was a man of knowledge. What Vivekananda said about Ramakrishna was said through the mirror of Vivekananda. It was never authentic. It couldn't be.

This has always been happening. It will go on happening. Buddha attracts persons who are the polar opposite to him. Mahavira and Jesus attract persons who are spiritually the other sex. These opposites then create the organization, the order. They will interpret. The very disciples will be the falsifiers. But this is what is so. It cannot be helped.

# II / *Right Questioning*

**Do not ask theoretical questions**, because theories solve less and confuse more. If there are no theories, there will be fewer problems. So it is not that theories solve questions or problems. On the contrary, questions arise out of theories.

And do not ask philosophical questions because philosophical questions simply *seem* to be questions. They are not questions. That's why no answer has been possible. If a question is really a question then it is answerable. If a question is false, just a linguistic confusion, then it cannot be answered. That's why philosophy has been answering and nothing has been answered. Philosophers go on answering continuously for centuries and centuries, and the questions remain the same. So howsoever you answer a philosophical question, you never answer it, because the question is false. The question was not meant to be answered at all; intrinsically the question is such that no answer is possible.

For example, if you ask who created the world, then it is something unanswerable. It is absurd. And do not ask metaphysical questions, not because they are not real questions – they are real questions – but they cannot be answered. Their realm is of the beyond. So you can question but they cannot be answered. They can be solved, but they cannot be answered.

Ask questions which are personal, intimate, existential. That is, one must be aware of what one is questioning and enquiring of – whether it is something which really means something to you. If it is answered, will a new dimension open for you? Will something be added to your existence? Will your being in any way be transformed through it? Really, is it something which you needed to have answered? Only such questions are religious.

Religion is really concerned with problems, not simply with questions. A question can be only a curiosity, but a problem is something intimate, personal, in which you are involved. It is *you*. A question is something separate from you; a problem – it is you. So before asking, dig deep inside and ask something that is intimate and personal, in which you are confused, in which you are involved. Only then can you be helped.

So now begin.

*Osho,*
*I have many confusions, but my main one is that I would like to know if everything I do is premeditated, my whole life. No matter what I do is there a certain course that it will take. Do I have any hand in it? – there is confusion.*

**It is both: yes and no both.**

*I would like to know if our lives are predestined or not?*

**It is both – yes and no both –** and it is always so with living problems. In a way you are determined – in a way. Whatsoever is physical in you, whatsoever is material in you, whatsoever is mental in you, is determined. And everything has a cause somewhere and is predictable. But still something in you constantly remains undetermined, and is unpredictable, and that is your consciousness.

So it depends. If you are identified with your body and your material existence much too much, then in the same proportion you are determined by causes. Then you are a machine, a biological machine. But if you are not identified with your material bodily existence, mind and body both included – if you can feel yourself something separate, different, above, transcending, then that transcending consciousness is never determined. It is spontaneous, free. Consciousness means freedom, and matter means non-freedom. Matter is the realm of slavery; consciousness is the realm of freedom. So it depends on you, how you define yourself. If you said, "I am only the body," then I would say yes, you are determined completely.

So a person who says that man is only a body cannot then say that man is not predetermined. This may seem very strange, because ordinarily, persons who don't believe in consciousness, don't believe in determination. And ordinarily persons who are religious and believe in consciousness believe in predetermination. So whatsoever I am saying will look very contradictory. But I say this is the case.

A person who has known consciousness has known freedom. So only a spiritual person can say there is no determination at all, but that realization comes only when you are completely unidentified with bodily existence. So who you are – if you feel yourself to be just a material existence, then no freedom is possible. With matter, freedom is impossible. Matter means that which cannot be free. It must flow in the chain of cause and effect. That's why I say both, and it will depend on you.

Once someone has achieved consciousness, enlightenment, he is completely out of cause and effect, and becomes unpredictable, absolutely unpredictable. You cannot say anything about him. He begins to live each moment; to say it in other words, his existence becomes atomic.

Your existence is a chain, a river-like chain, in which every step is determined from the past. Really your future is not future; it is just a by-product of the past. Your future is no future at all. It is only the past with the mind shaping, formulating, cultivating, conditioning. So your future – that's why your future is predictable.

In America there is a modern thinker and psychologist, B. F. Skinner. He also says that man is as predictable as anything. The main difficulty is not that man is unpredictable, it is that we have not yet devised implements to know his whole past. So the moment we know his past we can predict – everything is predictable. And he is right in a way. All the persons he has been working with in his labs are such. No buddha has come to his lab to be experimented upon, so he is right. He has been experimenting on hundreds and hundreds of people and he sees that they are all mechanical devices; nothing is there which can be called freedom.

But he is wrong because the study is limited, and even if only one person is free, it makes no difference – the whole theory falls down. It makes no difference if even only one person in the whole history of man is free and unpredictable, man is free and unpredictable.

But the whole thing will depend on the emphasis: whether you emphasize your body or you emphasize your consciousness. Where do you belong? Where are you belonging? – in the body or in the consciousness? Are you just an outward flow of life? – then everything is determined. Are you something inside also? But don't give any preformulated answer to it. Don't say, "Yes, I am a soul inside." Don't say it. If you feel that "there is nothing inside me," then be honest, because honesty is going to be the first step toward the inner freedom of consciousness.

So say, "I have no inside," if you feel that there is no inside. And really, if you go in, you will feel that everything is just part of the outside: your body has come from without, your thoughts have come from without, your self is being given to you by others. That's why you are so fearful of other's opinion – because they can withdraw your self completely. They may say, "You are a good man." But if you don't behave according to them they can withdraw their opinion and you will be poorer, and your "good" self will be nowhere.

That's why everyone is in fear, constant fear of others, because they are the contributors of your self. They can withdraw; at least they can withdraw their contribution. Your self is a contribution from others, your body is a contribution from others, your thoughts are a contribution from others, so where is the inside? You are just layers and layers of outside accumulation. If you are identifying with this personality, then everything is determined.

So unless one becomes aware of everything that comes

## Right Questioning

from the outside and goes on continuously not identifying with it, a moment comes where you don't find anything to reject. When you don't find anything to reject, you have come into a vacuum. This vacuum is the passage between the outside and the inside; this is the door. But we fear the vacuum. We are afraid of being empty so we cling to the outside accumulation.

So one has to be courageous enough to non-identify, and then to remain in the vacuum where there is no outside. When the outside falls completely you will be in a vacuum. If you are not courageous enough to be in the vacuum, you will again go out and cling to something, and be filled with it. So this moment is meditation, this "vacuum moment." If you are courageous enough, and if you can remain in this vacuum, soon your whole being will turn inside automatically, because when there is nothing to be attached to from the outside, your being turns inward. Then you know for the first time that you are something which transcends all that you have been thinking yourself to be.

Now you are something different from becoming; now you are being. This being is free; nothing can determine it. It is absolute freedom. No cause, no effect chain is possible here. So once a person begins to live "in" he becomes atomic. His actions now have a different correlation.

Ordinarily our actions are related with past actions. They come in a series: $A$, $B$, $C$. $A$ was a past act; it created a situation in which $B$ became possible; then $B$ became a past act associated with $A$, then it created a situation in which $C$ became a possibility, and it flowers. So your acts have a chain with other past acts, and this goes to the beginningless beginning and to the endless end. Not only your acts.

Your father and mother, their acts have a continuity with you. Not only your father and mother, your society, your history – all that has happened before you – is somehow interrelated with your act, that is happening this moment. The whole history has come to flower in you.

Everything that has ever happened is connected with your act, so your act is obviously determined – because your act is just such a minute part and the whole history is such a vital living force. You cannot determine it; it will determine you.

That's why Marx said, "It is not consciousness which determines conditions of society. It is society and society conditions which determine consciousness. It is not that great men create great societies." Marx says, "It is great societies which create great men." And he is right in a way, because as far as acts are concerned, you are not the owner; the whole history is the owner. You are just carrying something.

For example, you are carrying biological cells in you. They can become persons, but those cells are not yours. They've been given to you, not by someone, but by the whole biological evolution. The whole evolution has made your biological cell, which will give birth to a child. So you can be in a blissful ignorance that you are the father. You have been just a saint through which the whole history has acted, the whole biological evolution has acted, and has forced you to act. That's why sex is so forceful. It is beyond you.

So this is one way, how acts happen in relation to other past acts, in relation to past. But when a person becomes enlightened, then a new phenomena begins to happen. Any act is *not* connected with a past act; any act is connected with the person, with his consciousness. Now it comes from his consciousness. It is not from a past act. That's why you

## Right Questioning

cannot predict it – because past acts are known. If I have seen you angry in many situations, I can predict that in *this* situation you will be angry.

Skinner says that we can determine; I have seen your thirst so the thirst can be created. Skinner says that the old proverb has gone wrong now, that you can bring the horse to the river but you cannot force him to drink. Skinner says we can force him to drink, we can create the situation. We can create the situation; we can make the whole atmosphere so hot that the horse has to drink, and we know when he drinks, so we can create the situation and then the act will follow.

So I would say yes, the proverb has gone wrong, that you can bring the horse to the river but you cannot force him to drink. The horse can be forced, and you can also be forced, because your acts are situational. But I say you can bring a buddha to the river, you cannot force him to drink. Really, the more you force him, the more it will be impossible; exactly the contrary will happen. He can drink, but if you force him he will not. No heat will do, even if you bring a thousand suns around him it will not help, it will not help. On the contrary it will become impossible – more and more impossible – because now the person has a different origin of his acts. It is not connected with other acts. It is directly connected with consciousness.

That's why I emphasize so much: act consciously! Then, by and by, when you act consciously your acts change their total organization; the whole crystallization is different. It becomes associated with consciousness and not with acts. Then you are free. Then every moment *you* act; not that acts create other acts. *You* act. You begin to act, and no one can say how you will act, because habits are mechanical, consciousness is not. Habits are mechanical and by that I mean that habits repeat themselves. And the more you repeat, the more efficient you become in repetition.

So this must be understood: the more you repeat, the more you become efficient, and what do you mean by being efficient? By being efficient is meant that now no more consciousness is needed. A person who is an efficient typist – what do you mean by an efficient typist? You mean that now no conscious effort is needed. He can do it unconsciously, even with closed eyes. He can continue with other thoughts, he can sing, he can smoke and the typing continues. Now typing has gone to the unconscious center of the body. Now the body is typing; the man is not needed. That is efficiency. Efficiency means the thing is so determined that no error is possible. In freedom, error is possible. No machine *is*; it cannot err, because to err, one has to be conscious.

So acts can have a chain relationship with your other acts. Then they are determined. Then your childhood determines your youth, and your youth determines your old age, and everything is determined. Your birth determines your death. Buddha continues saying, he repeated so many times, "Given this, this happens. Provide the cause, and the effect will be there." This is the world of cause and effect in which everything is determined. You may know it or you may not know it.

Another crystallization of acts is with consciousness. Then it is moment to moment, because consciousness is a flow. It is not a static thing; it is life itself. It changes. It is alive. It goes on expanding. It goes on becoming new and fresh and young. It is never the past. It is always the present, so the act will be spontaneous.

# Right Questioning

I remember a Zen story...

A Zen master asks his disciple a particular question. The question is answered exactly as it should be answered.

Another day, and the master asks again, again the same question, and the disciple says, "But I have answered this one just the other day, I have answered it."

"But," the master says, "now I am asking again." The disciple repeats the answer, and the master says, "You don't know!"

"But," the disciple says, "yesterday I answered in the same way – those were the words exactly – and you nodded your head, and I interpreted that it was right. But why have you now changed your mind?"

The master said, "Anything that can be repeated is not coming from you. Anything that can be repeated is not coming from you. This answer has come from your memory, not from your consciousness. Memory is of the past. If you have really known, the answer would have differed, because so much has gone on, so much has changed. I am not the same man who asked you the other day. My emphasis is different, my eyes are different, the whole situation is different. You are different, but the answer is the same. You don't know the answer. And just to see whether you would repeat it, I had to ask again. Nothing can be repeated."

The more alive you are, the less repetitive. Only a dead man can be consistent. Life is inconsistency because life is freedom. Freedom cannot be consistent. Consistent with what? – with the past.

So an enlightened person is consistent only with his

consciousness and never with the past. He is always totally with his act. Nothing is left behind; nothing has been left. He is totally in it but it is momentary, it is atomic. The next moment the act has gone, the consciousness has gone back in again. It will come up again when any situation arises, and the act is going to be free again – as if this man is for the first time in this situation, he has never been in this situation before.

So that's why I say yes and no both. It depends on you – whether you are consciousness, or you are just an amalgamated, constituted, bodily existence.

Religion gives freedom because religion gives consciousness. Science will continue to grow more and more into slavery because science is concerned with matter. So the more science knows about matter, the more the world will be enslaved, because the whole phenomena is of cause and effect. If they know that given this, this happens, then everything can be determined.

Sooner – very soon – sooner than this century ends, we will see humanity being determined in so many ways. It is already being determined. Now the state knows very well how to determine you, how to create a stimulus response, how to create the stimulus and the response will follow. The greatest calamity that is possible is not the hydrogen bomb. It can only destroy. The real calamity will come from the psychological sciences, and that will be how to determine the human being completely. And it can be determined because we are not conscious – so we can be determined. Still as we are, we are determined. Someone is a Hindu; this is a determination. This is not freedom. Someone is a Mohammedan; this is a determination.

## Right Questioning

Parents are deciding; society is deciding. Someone is a doctor and someone is an engineer – this is a determination, someone has determined.

So we are being determined constantly, but our methods are still very primitive. But now, now new techniques can determine to such an extent that really it can then be said that there is no soul. If your every response – each and every response – is determined, then what is the meaning of calling yourself a soul?

All of this can be determined through body chemistry. If alcohol is given to you, you behave differently. Your body chemistry is different so you behave differently. Your behavior can be determined by alcohol.

In the old Tantra, the ultimate technique was to give intoxicants and still be conscious, to take intoxicants and still be conscious. When a person was still conscious when everything was bound to be unconscious, only then Tantra would say that now this man is enlightened, otherwise not – because if body chemistry can change your consciousness, what is the meaning? If just an injection can make you unconscious, then what is the meaning? Then that injection, that chemical drug, is more important, more powerful than your own consciousness, than your soul and everything. So it was a very daring experiment, but it is possible, it is possible to transcend every intoxicant drug and be conscious. Then the stimulus is given, but the response is not there; the condition is given, but the effect is not conditioned.

In every way, in every moment, in every act, act consciously more and more. But if something is given from the outside then we become more aware; something flows inside. But from the inside, we are not aware. For example sex. It is just…just a chemical phenomenon; some hormones floating in the body. A particular quantity of a particular hormone creates sexual desire in you. When it is created you are no longer there. You become the desire. You may repent when the hormones have gone, you may repent when the chemistry has come back to the ordinary level, but it is meaningless. This repentance is meaningless because again the hormones will be there and again you will act the same. Tantra also experimented with sex: given the whole situation – no sexual desire, then you are free. Somewhere, now, chemistry will be left far behind. Now the body will be there; you are not the body.

Anger also is chemistry and nothing else. So soon chemists will be able, particularly biochemists, to make you anger-proof. Just as a watch is waterproof, a man can be anger-proof or sex-proof. Some bodily change in the chemistry can be done and you will be anger-proof, but you will not be a Buddha. You will be anger-proof but you will not be a Buddha, because the difference will be Buddha was not incapable of anger – he was capable. Given the situation, the biological effect will not be there – you will be incapable of being angry. The biological situation is not, so the effect is not.

If your sex hormones are thrown out of the body you will not be sexual, but you will not *be*. So the real thing is how to be aware in a situation which requires your unawareness, how to be conscious in a situation which happens only in unconsciousness.

So whenever there is any such situation, meditate in it. You have been given a great opportunity. If you feel jealousy, meditate in it because this is the moment. Body chemistry is working around you. It will give you unconsciousness; you will behave as if you are mad. Now be conscious. Let there be jealousy; don't suppress it. Let there be jealousy, but be conscious; be a witness to it.

There is anger; be a witness to it. There is sex; be a witness to it. Let the body do whatsoever it is that is happening there. Begin to meditate in the whole situation. And by and by, the more the awareness is deepened, the less is the possibility of your being determined. You become free. And *moksha*, freedom, doesn't mean anything else. It means only consciousness so free that nothing can determine it.

You can ask anything you would like to ask.

*Osho,*
*Can you explain what divine love is? Or rather, what is love experienced in a divine way?*

**First take the question** – whether the question is determined by the immediate moment or the question was always ready in your mind; you were just waiting to ask it.

It was ready – because it cannot come just now, so it is determined. It was ready. You had decided it. It was waiting to be asked. It was forcing you to ask. So your memory has determined it, not your consciousness. If you are conscious in this moment, then this question cannot come in this way. It would have taken a completely different shape. It would have been qualitatively different, because whatsoever I have been saying, if you were here, immediately present to it, then this question would have been impossible.

And another thing, if this question was present in you, it is impossible to hear, because it must continue knocking to find an opportunity to ask, to be asked. So this question being constantly present in the mind will create a tension and because of this tension you will not be able to be immediately here. And that's why your consciousness cannot act atomically, with freedom. The question comes from mental bondage. So understand this first and then we can take the question.

The question in itself is not bad. It is good, very good, but your mind, working with it, has been ill. This is how awareness has to be worked out moment to moment, not only in acts, but in questions, and every gesture. If I raise this finger, it can be both. It can be just a habit. If it is just a habit, then I am not the master of my body at all. It may be a spontaneous expression of something that is present in my consciousness just now, then it is altogether different.

If you go to a Christian preacher, then his every gesture is also predetermined. He has been taught. He has passed through a training. I happened to be in a theological college once, a Christian theological college, so I just walked around. They were training preachers, a five year course, then they would become D.D., Doctors of Divinity. Absurdity! No one can be a doctor of divinity. And even if you can be a doctor of divinity then nothing, nothing is of value. With a five year course one can become a doctor of divinity! One can become a doctor of chemistry, that is okay. It means something. But a doctor of divinity is sheer idiocy.

So I went around and I saw that everything was being taught there. They were trained in everything: how to stand at the pulpit, how to begin, how to raise the hymn, how to look at the audience, where to stop and where to give a gap, and an interval. Everything! This must not happen. This is a misfortune if it happens.

## Right Questioning

So be aware that the question was present, knocking at the mind continuously. You were not hearing at all. Whatsoever was being said has not been heard – and only because of this question. And one thing more, when I am talking about your question, the same mind will create another question and that will continue to knock at your mind. And you will miss again because the mind works repetitively, in a mechanical way. It will provide you with another question. And this is not to you personally, but to everyone. It makes no difference that you have asked and others have not asked. It makes no difference.

Now the question. It is difficult for me to say that anything such as divine love exists, because love is divine. Whenever it exists it is divine, wherever it exists it is divine. So to say "divine love" is meaningless. Love is divine, but we are cunning, the mind is cunning. It says: "We know what love is. The only thing that we don't know is divine love."

We don't even know love. Love is one of the most unknown things. Too much talk, never lived – and really this is a trick of the mind. The thing which we cannot live, we talk about more and more.

So love is the only theme around which literature, music, poetry, dance – everything happens around it. And inside there is nothing. If there is really love, then there will be no talk about it. We talk only about things which we lack. This talking too much about love means love is non-existential. This is how mind works. We talk about things which are not. We never talk about things which are. This talking about things which are not is just a substitution method. That which is not – we create an illusion by talking, by language, by symbols, by art. We create a facade, an illusion, that the thing is there. You can write a very good poem about love, and you have not known love at all. And it is possible that one who has not known love may write a better poem, because the vacuum is much deeper in him. It has to be filled, substituted. So the first thing: love is lacking, love is not there.

So it is better to understand what love is, because when you ask what divine love is, it is understood that love is known. Love is not known. So whatsoever is known as love is something else. And the false must be known before some steps toward the real, toward the true.

What is known as love is not love, but infatuation. Infatuation. That infatuation is not known in animals, so we think that love is something human, because animals don't know anything like…such as love – they know sex. But this is the problem. Animals don't know anything like love; they know sex very well. So is love something new to human mind? Are there some flaws?

There is some flaw. You begin to love someone; if that someone is given to you totally, love will soon die. If there are barriers, and you cannot achieve the person you love, you cannot get the person you love, love will develop. It will become intense. The more the barriers, the more intense the love will be felt. If the beloved or the lover is such that he is impossible to get, then love will become eternal. If you can get your lover easily, easily dies the love. So what is the reason?

When you try to get something and you are not getting it, you become tense about getting it. The more there are barriers and hindrances, the more your ego feels to do something. It becomes an ego problem. Tension is created. The ego comes in and takes over the tension. The more you are denied, the

## Right Questioning

more tense, the more complex, the more infatuated. This you call "love," this tension. That's why, if you are married to your lover, the honeymoon is over, the love is over. Even before, because all that you knew as love was not love. It was just infatuation, ego infatuation, ego tension – a struggle, a conflict, aggression, malice, resolve.

The old human societies, ancient human societies, were very cunning. They devised methods to make your love last long. So if a person cannot see his wife in the daylight, the love will be long. If he cannot meet her often – even with his wife – if he cannot meet her, then even his own wife holds an infatuation and tension is created. Then one man can remain with one wife his whole life, and can die praying to God that the same wife should be given to him again.

In the West, marriage cannot exist anymore. It is not that the Western mind is more sexual. No. The only thing is the infatuation is not allowed to accumulate. Sex is so easily available that marriage cannot exist. Love too cannot exist with this kind of freedom. If you make a completely free sexual society, then only sex can exist. And it will come to the very level as animals are. But by that I don't mean that you have gone somewhere else; you simply think that you have gone somewhere, the level remains the same. The whole thing is illusory.

This infatuation is bound to create boredom because boredom is the second side, the other side of infatuation. If you love someone and don't get the loved one, infatuation goes deep. If you get it, then the other side comes in. You begin to get bored, fed up. And there are many dualisms: infatuation/boredom, love/hate, attraction/repulsion. With infatuation you will feel attraction, you will feel love. With boredom you will feel repulsion, you will feel hate. This is how things are.

No attraction can be love because repulsion is bound to come. It is in the very nature of things. The other side will come. If you don't want that the other side should come, then you must create barriers, such barriers in which the infatuation never ends – the infatuation continues, so that the other side is not known. You must create daily tensions, then it continues. This is the whole old system of creating a facade of love.

Now it will not be possible, and if it will not be possible then with marriage love will also go down. Really, it has gone in the West, it has gone. Sex remains. And then, sooner or later, sex alone cannot stand. Then it becomes so mechanical, so physical.

Nietzsche declared only seventy years before that God is dead. But the real thing that is going to be dead is sex. And with this century sex will be completely dead. I don't mean by that that people will become non-sexual. They will be sexual, but the infatuation, the significance, the too-much emphasis on it will go. It will become an act just as ordinary as anything – as urination, or food, or anything. It will not be meaningful. It became meaningful because of the barriers and the infatuation – and this you have been calling love.

This is not love. This is just sex delayed, just sex delayed. Then what is love? Love is a very different dimension. Really it is not related with sex at all – really. Sex may come in, may not come in; it is not really related with sex at all. It has a different being of its own.

To me, love is a by-product of a meditative mind. It is not really related with sex. It is related with *dhyana*, it is related with meditation, because the more silent you become, the more at ease with yourself, the more fulfilled you feel, a new expression of your being takes place. You begin to love. Not for someone particularly – it may happen, it may happen even particularly, that is another thing – but you begin to love. This loving becomes just your way of existing. Then there is no other side. Then it can never turn into repulsion because it is not attraction at all.

You must understand the distinction exactly. When I fall in love with someone ordinarily, really, the feeling is not that love is flowing from me toward him; the real feeling is how to possess him. It is not that something is going from me to him. Rather it is an expectation that something will come from him to me. That's why love becomes possession: possess someone so that you can get something out of him. But the love I am talking about is neither possession nor with any expectations. It is just how you behave. You have become so silent that the silence goes to others.

When you are angry, anger goes to others. When you are in hate, hate goes to others. When you are in love, the so-called love, you feel love is going to others. But you are not dependable, reliable. This moment there is love, the next moment there will be hate. And don't think that that hate is something opposite to your love. It is just part and parcel of it; a continuity.

If you have loved someone, you will hate him. You may not be courageous enough to recognize it, or to say it, or to confess it, but you will hate. So see lovers: always in conflict if they are together. When they are not together they may be singing about each other, but when they are together they are just fighting. They cannot live alone, they cannot live together – because when they are alone, the other fails.

Infatuation is created because the other is not available; then infatuation is there, then they feel again love. When the other is present, the infatuation is gone; they feel hatred.

The love I am talking about means you have become so silent that now there is neither anger nor attraction nor repulsion. Really, now there is no love, no hate. Really, now you are not other-oriented at all, at all! The other has disappeared; you are alone with yourself. In this feeling of aloneness, love comes to you just as a fragrance. Love is a fragrance when someone is alone, totally alone.

To ask for the other is always ugly. To depend on the other is always possessive. To ask something from the other, will always creates bondage and suffering, and conflict. A person who is sufficient unto himself – that's what I mean by meditation. It is being sufficient unto oneself. You have become a circle, alone. The mandala is complete.

You are trying to make the mandala complete with others: man with woman, woman with man. Trying to make the circle complete. In certain moments the lines meet, but they have not even met when the separation sets in – and you are again half. If you become a whole inside, a circle – complete, sufficient, no line going outward, nothing going outward to the other, a perfect circle inside – then something begins to flower in you which is love. Then whosoever comes near you, you love him. It is not an act at all. It is not that you "do" love to him. It is not any doing at all. It is that your very being, your very presence is love. Love flows through you.

If you ask such a person, "Do you love me?" he will be in a very difficult situation. He cannot say, "I love you," because it is not an act on his part. It is no "doing" to him. He

## Right Questioning

cannot say, "I do not love you," because he loves. Really, he *is* love.

This love comes only with the freedom I have been talking of. So freedom is your feeling, and love is the others' feeling about you. When this meditation happens inside, freedom is your feeling – that I am free, completely free. This is your freedom, this is your feeling. No one else will be able to feel it because this is something very in. How can anyone else feel it? Your freedom cannot be felt by others.

Sometimes your behavior may create only difficulties for them, but they cannot conceive of what has happened in you. And in a way you will become difficult for them. In a way you will be a trouble, an inconvenience, because you cannot be predicted. Nothing can be known about you: what you will do, what you will say, what is going to happen in the next moment. No one can know. Then everyone becomes inconvenienced around you. Your freedom can only be felt in this way by others – that you become inconvenient to them. They can never be at ease with you. That is the only feeling they get because you may do anything; you are not dead.

But they cannot feel your freedom – and how can they feel it? They have not known it. They have not even enquired into it, they have not sought it, they have not been on any search. And they are in such a bondage. They cannot even conceive of what freedom is. They have been in cages. They have not known the open sky, so even if you talk about the open sky it will be incommunicable, it will not be communicated to them.

But they can feel your love, because they have asked for it always and always. Even in their cages they have been searching for love; even in their bondage. Really they have created the whole bondage because they have been asking for love. They have created the whole bondage – the bondage with persons, the bondage with things. They have been creating it only in the search for love.

So whenever a person happens to be free, his love is felt. But you will feel that love as compassion, not as love, because there will be no excitement in it. It will be a very diffused light – with no heat, not even warmth. If we can phrase "cold love" then it will be meaningful.

You cannot say Buddha's love is warm – you cannot say that. It is ice cool. There is no excitement in it. It is there, that's all, because no excitement can be a part of your being. Excitement comes and goes; it cannot be constant. So if there is excitement in love then Buddha will have to go into hate again and again. Excitement will not be there, peaks will not be there; then valleys will be there. So he is neither a peak nor a valley; he is just a plain. The love is ice cool so you will feel it as compassion, as *karuna*.

This is the difficulty. Freedom cannot be felt from the outside; only love can be felt and that too as compassion. And this has been one of the very difficult phenomena of human history, because their freedom creates inconvenience and their love compassion – so human society is always divided about these people.

A Christ: someone has felt only the inconvenience that he has created – and these will be the people who are well settled, because they don't need any compassion. These will be the people who are well settled, who think that they have got love and health, wealth, respect, everything. So when Christ happens, the "haves" will be against him because he will be creating only inconvenience for them, and the

# Right Questioning

"have-nots" will be with him because they will feel his compassion. They are in need of love. No one has loved them; this man loves them. They will not feel the inconvenience because they have nothing by which to feel the inconvenience – they have nothing to lose.

So when this man dies everyone will feel his compassion, because now there is no inconvenience; there is no inconvenience. Even the settled ones, the conformists, will feel at ease. They will worship him. But when he is living, he is a rebel. He is a rebel not because there is something wrong in society. He is a rebel because he is free.

You must understand: he is not a rebel because there is something wrong in the society. Those rebellions are only political. So if a society changes, the very one who was a rebellious one will become an orthodox one. This happened in 1917. The same revolutionaries became one of the most anti-revolutionary cliques in the world. A Stalin or a Mao, they become the most anti-revolutionary leaders the moment they are in power because they are not rebellious; they were rebelling only against a particular situation. The situation gets thrown over, now they are in the same saddle.

But a Christ is always rebellious. No situation will do it. No situation will help his rebellion to lessen. The rebellion will never be less because the rebellion is not against anyone. It is because he has a free consciousness. So anywhere he feels the barrier, he will be rebellious. Rebellion is his spirit. So even if Jesus comes today, Christians will not be at ease with him. They cannot be. They will behave in the same manner as Jews behaved with him; now they are settled. The pope cannot behave otherwise; he is settled. And a Jesus again in the marketplace will disturb the whole thing. Rome will not be. With Jesus Rome is not possible, with Jesus the pope is not possible; only without Jesus is he possible.

But compassion is also felt. That's one thing more to be understood. That's why every teacher who has known is a rebellious teacher, but the tradition that is connected with him is never rebellious. It is only concerned with his compassion. It is never concerned with his rebellion, never concerned with his freedom, only with his love. Then it becomes impotent because love cannot exist without freedom; love cannot exist without rebellion.

You cannot be as loving as Buddha unless you are as free as Buddha. So a Buddhist monk is just trying to be in compassion, but then compassion is impotent because the freedom is not there. And the freedom is the source. A Mahavira is in compassion, but a Jaina monk is not in compassion at all. He just tries, he is just trying to act nonviolence and compassion, etcetera, but he is not compassion at all. He is cruel in every way; cunning, crooked, in every way. Even in his compassion and its exhibition, he is cunning. There is no compassion at all, because the freedom is not there.

So to me, whenever there is the happening of freedom in a consciousness, freedom is felt inside and love is felt outside. Then love is not opposite to hatred. It is just absence of both: hate and love. It is difficult, that is why I have to use the word *love* for both things. It is absence of both love and hate. The complete dualism is absent. It is absence of attraction and repulsion both.

So a person who is free and loving, it depends on you whether you can take his love or not. With us, it is not so. If I love you it is not on me how much I can take; it is always on you, how much you can give. Ordinarily we love, then the love depends on the person who is giving; he may not give. But when this love happens, then how much you can take is not dependent on the giver. It is dependant on you, because the giver is completely open and giving all the moment. Even when there is no one present, the love is flowing.

It is just like a flower – no one passing by, in a dense forest – a single flower. No one may even know about it, that it has flowered and is giving its perfume. But it will give it, because it is not being given *to* someone. It is just being given, by the very intrinsic happening. The flower has flowered so the fragrance is there. Someone may pass or not; it is irrelevant. If someone passes and is capable, is sensitive, he may get it. If someone passes and is completely dead, insensitive, he may not even be aware that there was a flower by the road, by the side.

So when love is there you can get it or not. When love is not there the other can give to you or not. And there is no division of divine or non-divine. Love is divine, so all we can say – love is divine, love is godliness.

So more tomorrow, hmm?

# 12 / *Balancing the Rational and the Irrational*

*Osho,
Could you comment on why the western youth are in revolt, and why so many young people from the West are now becoming interested in Eastern religion and philosophy? Do you have any particular message for the West?*

**Mind is a very contradictory system.** Mind works in polar opposites. But our thinking, our logical way of thinking, always chooses one part of it and denies the other. So logic proceeds in a non-contradictory way, and mind works in a contradictory way. Life works in opposites, and logic works in a linear way – not in opposites.

For example, you have both possibilities in the mind: to be angry to the extreme and to be silent also, to the extreme. If you can be angry it doesn't mean that you cannot be non-angry to the other

## Balancing the Rational and the Irrational

extreme also. If you can be disturbed, it doesn't mean that you cannot be silent. The mind goes on working in both ways. If you can be loving, you can be full of hatred also. One doesn't deny the other.

But in logic, in thinking, if we think that someone is loving, then we begin to think that he cannot be capable of hate. And we even begin to think about ourselves in this way also. This is a part. So if you go on loving then you begin to think that "I am incapable of hate," and then hate goes on accumulating inside. Then when you reach to a peak of your loving attitude, everything shatters and you fall down into hate. The individual mind not only works like that, the society's mind also.

For example, the West has come to the peak of rational thinking. Now the irrational part of the mind will take revenge. The irrational part of the mind has been denied expression, so for these last fifty years that irrational part of the mind has been taking revenge in so many ways: through art, through poetry, through drama, through literature, through philosophy, and now through living. So the revolt of the youth is really a revolt of the irrational part of the mind against too much rationality.

The East can be helpful because the East has lived the other part, the irrational. And the East has also reached to its peak. So now the Eastern youth is more interested in communism than in religion; the Eastern youth is more interested in rational thinking than in irrational living.

So as I see it, now the whole pendulum will turn. The East will become the West, and the West will become the East.

Whenever you reach to a peak of any part of the mind, you have to swing back. That's how history works. So in the West, now meditation will be more meaningful. Poetry will gain a new hold and science is bound to decline. So the modern youth will be anti-technological and ultimately anti-scientific. And the modern youth of the West will be anti-culture also, and anti-civilization. This is just a natural working.

And we have not yet been able to develop a personality which is comprehensive of both parts – neither in the East nor in the West. We have always chosen parts – part of the mind – and then we go and develop in that part and the other remains hungry, starved. And then there is bound to be rebellion and the whole thing will shatter, and the mind will move to the other side. This has been the whole working of our history, in both the West and in the East; this has been the dialectics.

So now, for the West, meditation is more meaningful than thinking because meditation means no-thinking. So Zen will be more appealing, Buddhism will be more appealing, yoga will be more appealing. These are all irrational attitudes toward life. They don't emphasize conceptualizations, they don't emphasize theories, theologies. They emphasize a zest to go deep into existence, not into thinking. So I think that the more technology develops and the more the hold of the mind begins to become a grip on the neck, the more the other will be coming.

So in the West, the revolt of the younger generation is very meaningful and very significant – very significant. It is a historical point of a change, a change of the whole consciousness. Now the West cannot continue as it has been. It cannot continue; a point of deep crisis has come, a cul-de-sac. You cannot go further. You have to move in some other direction because now for the first time a society is affluent.

Individuals have been affluent, never a whole society. Now

## Balancing the Rational and the Irrational

a whole society is affluent. And whenever a society becomes affluent, riches lose meaning. Riches are only meaningful in a poor society. Affluence is significant in a poor society. Even there, whenever someone becomes really affluent he is bored. A Buddha is bored because of his family affluence; he is just bored. The more sensitive a person is, the sooner he becomes bored. A Buddha is bored; he leaves everything.

Now Buddha appeals to the West and the whole attitude of the modern youth is just of empty affluence. They are leaving, and they will go on leaving unless the whole society becomes poor. They will go on leaving unless the whole society becomes poor, because this leaving movement, this renunciation, can exist only in an affluent society. But if it goes to the extreme, then the society declines. Then technology will have no progress, and if this goes on, then in the West you will create the East.

And in the East now they are turning to the other extreme; they will create a West. Really, if we can read the future, then the East is just turning into the West. It is difficult to see the future, but the footsteps can be heard – and the West is turning toward the East. But the disease remains the same because as I see it, the disease is the bifurcation of the mind.

We have never allowed the human mind to flower in its totality. We have always chosen one part against the other, at the cost of the other. This has been the whole misery. We have not accepted the totality of the human mind.

So I am neither Eastern nor Western. I am against both. I am against both because I say that these are partial attitudes – so sometimes one may appeal to you but the appeal is partial and it cannot, cannot help to grow a totality, a total mind.

So to me neither the East is the choice nor the West; they

both have failed. The East has failed by choosing religion and the West is failing by choosing science. Unless we choose both, now there is no going out of this vicious circle.

We can change, we *can* change – and this is strange. If you talk about Buddhism in Japan no young one is ready to listen. They are after technology and the Western youth is after Zen Buddhism. In India, the newer generation is not in the least interested in religion. They are more interested in economics, more interested in politics, more interested in technology, engineering, science – everything except religion.

And the Western youth is not really interested in technology now. They are not interested in science, in progress. They are interested in living here and now. They are not interested in future utopias – socialism, etcetera – not interested. The avante-garde of the youth in the West is interested in religion; the avante-garde of the youth in the East is interested in science. And this is just changing the burden – and then again the same fallacy.

My interest is with the total mind. I am interested in the total mind – how a human mind is possible; a mind which is neither Eastern nor Western, but just human – a global mind. And this is a very difficult problem, because it is very easy to live with one part of the mind. You can live neatly, cleanly, mathematically. If you want to live with both parts of the mind, then you have to live a very inconsistent life. Inconsistent, of course, superficially, but on a deeper layer you have a consistency, a spiritual harmony.

And as I see it, a man remains poor spiritually unless he has the opposite polarity also. Then you become rich.

For example, if you are simply an artist and you have no scientific mind, your art is bound to be poor. It cannot have the richness, because the richness comes only with the opposite in it. Just like right now we have only males in this room – then the room lacks something. The moment females enter, the room becomes spiritually rich. Now the polar opposites are here, and the polar opposites make a greater whole.

So to me the mind must be able to move in a liquidity. It must not be fixed anywhere. A mathematician can be a rich mathematician if he can move into the worlds of art. These worlds are quite non-mathematical, even anti-mathematical. But if the mathematician can move, if his mind has a freedom to move from fixations, then back to mathematics, he will be a richer mathematician – because through the opposite, a cross-breeding happens, and through the opposite you begin to look at things in so many different dimensions, that the total perspective is bound to be richer.

So to me a person must have a religious mind with a scientific training, or a scientific mind with religious discipline. And I see no inherent impossibility in it. Rather on the contrary, I think the mind will become more alive if you can move. So to me, meditation means a deep movement: a freedom from fixations.

For example, if I become too logical then I become incapable of understanding poetry. Logic becomes a fixation. Then when I read poetry, or listen to poetry, the fixation begins to work. Then the poetry looks absurd, not because it is, but because I have a fixation with logic. And from the viewpoint of logic, poetry is absurd. If I become fixated with poetry then logic becomes just a utilitarian thing, with no depth in it, and I become closed.

And this has been happening all through history – every

period, every nation, every part of the world, every culture and society has always chosen a part and emphasized the part, and created a personality around it. The personality has been poor, lacking much. Neither the East has been rich spiritually nor the West. They cannot be. Richness comes through the opposite – an inner dialogue, an inner dialectics. So to me, neither the East is worth choosing nor the West. To me, a different mind, an altogether different quality of mind, has to be chosen – and that quality means one has to be at ease with oneself, without choosing.

For example a tree grows: we can choose; we can cut down all the branches and we can allow the tree to grow in only one direction, one branch growing. It will be a poor tree, very poor and very ugly, and ultimately the tree is bound to be in very deep difficulty because this branch cannot grow. It can grow only in a deep relationship with other branches. It can grow when in a family of branches. And a moment is bound to come when this branch will feel in a cul-de-sac. It cannot grow anymore. A tree, to be really rich and growing, must grow in all the directions, opposite directions. It must grow toward every direction. Only then will this tree be rich, strong, multidimensional.

To me, the human spirit must grow like a tree, in all directions. And the old conception must be dropped that we cannot grow in opposite directions. We *can* grow; really we can only grow when we grow in opposite directions. But up until now this has not been the case. Up until now we have tried a specialization in the human mind also – one should grow in one specific direction. Then something ugly happens. One grows in a specific direction, but then he lacks everything. He becomes one branch, not a tree, not a tree. And this

## Balancing the Rational and the Irrational

branch is also bound to be poor, bound to be poor.

Not only have we been cutting the branches of the mind, we have been cutting the roots. We allow only one root and one branch, so a very starved human being has come up all over the world. In the East, in the West, everywhere – very starved. And the East is always attracted toward the West and the West is attracted toward the East, because I am attracted to something which I lack, you are attracted to something which you lack. If you lack religion, whenever you feel starved you are attracted to the East. When the East begins to feel poor, poverty-stricken, diseased, ill, the East begins to be attracted toward the West, because of science, technology, affluence, medicine, everything.

Because of the body, the East begins to be attracted toward the West. And because of the spirit, the West begins to be attracted toward the East. But we can change positions and the disease remains the same. So it is not a question now of changing positions. It is now a question of changing the whole perspective. It is not a question of changing the East to the West. Now it is a question of changing the whole past into a new future.

The whole past has been a fragmentary choice of human possibilities. We have never accepted the whole being. Somewhere sex is not accepted; then we deny something. Somewhere, the world is not accepted; then we deny something. Somewhere, emotion is not accepted; then we deny something.

This denial has been the problem and we have never been so strong that we can accept everything that is human with no condemnation, and allow the human being to grow in every direction. And the more you grow in opposite directions, the greater will be the growth, and the richness, and the inner affluence. And abundance is bound to result.

So I have nothing specifically to say to the West or to the East. Whatsoever I have to say is to the human mind as such, to change the total perspective. The change is from the past to the future – not from this present to that present. And unless we see this it is difficult to have a new man, and the problem is *how* to have a new man.

The problem is colossal, arduous, because this fragmentation has become so deep-rooted. I cannot accept my anger, I cannot accept my sex, I cannot accept my body, I cannot accept myself in my totality. Somewhere something has to be denied and thrown away. Something is evil, something is bad, something is a sin. So I go on cutting branches and ultimately I am not a tree, not an alive thing, just dead, because this fear of growing into branches which I have denied…they can again come up. So I become fearful; everywhere suppressed and fearful. Then, a disease sets in: a sadness, a death.

So we go on living partial lives which are more near to death than to life. This acceptability of the total human potentiality, and bringing everything in it to its peak without feeling any inconsistency, any contradiction – really, if I cannot be authentically angry, I cannot be loving. But this has not been the attitude up to now. We have been thinking that a person is more loving if he is incapable of anger.

> *Supposing the tree is growing next to a wall. The wall is there. The branches cannot grow in all directions because a wall is there. The wall may be an existing society, may be an existing condition. How can that tree grow?*

## Balancing the Rational and the Irrational

**Yes I understand.** There are many walls. But those walls have been created by the trees, by no one else. There are walls, but those walls have not been imposed by someone else; by the trees, and the trees have been supporting those walls. So it is through their cooperation that the walls exist. The moment the trees are ready not to support them, not to build them, the walls will drop, they will shatter, they will just evaporate.

These walls that exist around the human race are our creation and we have created them because of some conceptions, some philosophic attitudes. We have created these walls because of the attitudes of our human mind. For example, I must teach my child not to be angry because of a conception that if he becomes angry or if he goes on feeling more anger, he will not be a loving child. So I create walls that he should not be angry – must suppress his anger – without knowing that if he suppresses his anger, simultaneously the capacity to love is destroyed. They are not opposite. They are two branches. If you cut one, the other becomes poor, because the same sap runs through all these branches.

So if I am to train my child for a better life, I will train him to be authentically angry. I will not say, "Don't be angry." I will say, "When you are angry, then be authentically and totally angry, and don't feel any guilt about anger." Rather than to say to him don't be angry, I will train him to be rightly angry. And whenever the moment is right, be angry authentically. Don't be angry when the wrong moment is there. And in the same way I will tell him when the right moment for love is there, be authentically in love; but when the wrong moment is there don't be in love.

So the question is not what to choose between anger and love. The question is between right and wrong. The anger must be given an expression. And a child is beautiful when really angry. An ardor comes to him, a beauty, a sudden flush of energy and life. If you kill the anger, then you are killing life. Then he will be just impotent his whole life. He cannot move, alive; he will move as a dead corpse.

So we say – we go on creating concepts which create the walls. We go on giving notions, ideologies which create the walls. These walls are not imposed on us; they are our creations. And the moment we become aware, the walls will disappear. They exist because of us.

> *But supposing that the tree, or the person is handicapped because of biological conditions? He cannot change, not because he doesn't want, but he can't. Or for instance, a mad person. How would you see the position of such a person?*

**Really, these are exceptions;** they are not problems. The problem is the non-exceptional common man. These exceptions are not problems. We can treat them. When the whole society is alive, when the whole society is alive we can treat them. We can analyze them. We can help them; they have to be helped. They cannot do anything by themselves, but even in their helplessness our society has a part. That part must be taken out.

For example, a son of a prostitute can never feel really free because of your society: the moral conception. He goes on feeling a deep guilt for which he is not responsible at all. Your society is responsible, because it was not his responsibility that his mother was a prostitute. How can he help it?

## Balancing the Rational and the Irrational

What can he do about it? But your society will go on behaving with the boy in a different way. His mother being a prostitute is not his responsibility at all. But unless we have a different attitude about sex, this prostitute guilt is bound to be there; it will continue, it will continue.

This prostitution becomes a guilt phenomenon because we have made marriage something sacred. If marriage is something sacred, then prostitution is bound to be something sinful. Unless marriage is brought down from the pedestal of sacredness, you cannot do anything. That is only a part, a part. And prostitution has existed because of your marriage system, and it will continue unless the whole marriage system changes. So prostitution is just a part of the whole marriage system.

Really, as the human mind is, a permanent relationship is unnatural. And a forced permanent relationship is really criminal. If I want to live with someone I can continue, but that must be my choice. That must not be the law. If it is a law, if it is forced on me, that if today I love someone – it is not in nature; there is no intrinsic necessity that the love will be there tomorrow also. It has no intrinsic naturalness about it. It may be; it may not be. And when you force it to be there, the more it becomes impossible. It will not be. Then prostitution comes from the back door. Unless we have a society with a free relationship, we cannot drop prostitution.

And if it continues, then you feel good because you are in a permanent relationship, and you have to feel good otherwise it may be difficult to be in a permanent relationship; your ego must be fulfilled. To fulfill your ego – that you are a faithful husband or a faithful wife – the prostitute has to be condemned. Then the son has to be condemned, and then it becomes a disease.

But these are exceptional cases – that someone is medically, physically wrong. Then we have to help him, then we have to treat him medically, psychologically. But the whole society is not like that. Ninety-nine percent of society is our creation; the one percent is the exception, that is not the problem at all. And it may dissolve if this ninety-nine percent of society changes – the one percent will be affected by it.

We cannot yet decide to what extent your physiology is determined by your mind. We are yet not certain and the more we know, the more we become uncertain. Many diseases in the body may be just because of a wrong mind. With a wrong mind you become more vulnerable, with a wrong mind you become more receptive to diseases. And we cannot know unless we have a free mind.

Really, so many diseases are really a human phenomenon. In animals they are not. Animals are more healthy; less diseased, less ugly. There is no reason why man cannot be more alive, more beautiful, more healthy. This training for ten thousand years, a wrong training of the mind, may be the root cause, may be the root cause.

And when you are in the pattern, you cannot even conceive, you cannot even conceive… Many physical diseases are just because of a wrong mind, of a crippled mind, and we are crippling everybody's mind. And now psychologists say that it becomes difficult if in the beginning – the first seven years of the child are the most significant. If you cripple the mind, then it becomes more and more difficult to change it. But we go on crippling, we go on killing and cutting, and with a very good conscience. And when you

## Balancing the Rational and the Irrational

do something wrong with a very good conscience, then it is a problem, then it is a problem.

The more psychology penetrates deep into the roots of the mind, the more parents seem to be criminals, but unknowingly; the more teachers and the whole educational system seem to be a criminality, but unknowingly – because they have also suffered from older generations and they are only passing on the diseases.

But now a possibility opens because for the first time in many parts of the world, particularly in the West, man is free from day-to-day needs; man is free from a long millennia of poverty. So now we can think, we can plan, we can change. We can experiment with the new possibilities of the mind. It was impossible in the past, impossible, because bodily needs were so heavy. There was no possibility, there was no possibility. But now the possibility opens and we live on a threshold of a very deep revolution – such a revolution as human history has never encountered. A revolution in consciousness is possible now. With more facilities to know and understand, we can change, we can change. It will take time, much time will be needed, but the possibility is open. And if we dare and if we have some courage, it can become an actuality.

Now the whole humanity is at stake. Either we will go back to the past or to a new future. So to me it is not a question of a third world war, not a question of communism and capitalism. Those problems are now just out of date. A new crisis, a very vital crisis is nearby. Either we will have to decide to have a new consciousness, and to work for it, or we have to fall back, regress to the old patterns.

This is also possible, that we may regress, because whenever – this is a tendency with the mind – whenever you face something which you cannot face, you regress. If we are here and suddenly the house is on fire, we begin to behave like children. We regress. We cannot do anything. We cannot do anything so we regress. We begin to behave like children. That may be dangerous because when the house is on fire you need more maturity. You need more understanding. You need to behave in a more aware way. But when the house is on fire you will regress to the age of five and you will begin to run in such a way that you may create more danger for yourself than the fire itself can create.

So that is also a very sad possibility, that because of facing such a new phenomenon – to create a new human being – we may regress, we may regress. And there are prophets who go on preaching regression. They always want the past, to go back: "It was better." Always, there are prophets who are the prophets of the dead past, who'll always say, "The golden age has been in the past so go back. Go back!" But to me that is suicidal. We must go toward the future, howsoever hazardous, and howsoever difficult and arduous.

Life must go toward the future. We must find new modes of existence. And I am hopeful that this can happen. And the West has to be the ground for its happening, not the East, because the East is just the West three hundred years back. So the East will have to follow the West – so many earthly problems so heavy upon it, but the West is free in a way.

So when hippies come to me, I am always aware that they can do both. They can just regress. In a way they are regressing, they are behaving like children, they are falling back. That is not good. They are falling back; they are behaving like primitives. That's not good. The revolt is good, but they must behave like new men, not like primitives. And they must create possibilities for a new consciousness.

But they are just drugging themselves, and through drugs the primitive mind has always been enchanted. The primitive mind has always been magically hypnotized by drugs. So if the new generation in the West begins to behave like primitives, it is not then rebellion, but a reaction and a regression. They must behave like the new humanity. And they must proceed toward a new consciousness which is total, global – an accepting of all the inconsistent potentialities within the being.

Really, that is the difference between animals and man. Animals have fixed potentialities, consistent. That is what they call their instincts. Man has no fixed potentiality – infinite possibilities, *only* possibilities. He can grow in many directions simultaneously. This growth must be helped, and we must create centers where this growth is helped with everything.

The mind must be trained in a logical, rational way. It must be trained simultaneously in the irrational, non-rational meditation. Their reason must be trained, and at the same time their emotion also. The reason must not be trained now at the cost of emotion. Their doubt must be healthy, but their faith also. This is the problem.

It is easy to be faithful without any doubt. It is easy. To be doubtful without any faith – it is easy, it is simple. But these simple formulas will not do now. We must create a healthy doubt, a persistent doubt, a skeptical mind simultaneously with a trusting, with a faithful mind. And the inner being must be capable of moving from doubt to faith. If something is – for example with any objective research – then the new man must be doubtful, skeptical, questioning, enquiring. But there is also another dimension of existence where trust gives the clues, not doubt. But both are needed.

So this is the problem: how to create the contradictory polarities simultaneously. And I am interested in this. So I go on creating doubt and go on creating faith. And I don't see any inner inconsistency in it, because to me the movement is meaningful, the movement from one pole to another.

But the more we are fixed to one pole, the more the movement becomes difficult. If we emphasize – for example, in the East we have never emphasized too much activity, so lethargy has been a part of the Eastern consciousness. So the East could sleep very well. Even when the East was not sleeping, it was sleepy. But in the West you have cultivated activity. Now the mind has become fixed. You cannot sleep, so sleep has to be drugged, forced, through tranquillizers or through something else. But still that forced sleep cannot give you sleep. It is not natural. It is just chemical and superficial, and deep down the turmoil goes on. So sleep has become just a nightmare: a chemical force surfaces there, but on the inside the split goes on. Why? You have emphasized activity too much so the mind becomes fixed. So when you go to sleep, it needs to move from activity to inactivity. It cannot move, becomes fixed. So you go on turning in your bed, but the mind cannot move from activities. It goes on being active.

And the opposite has happened in the East. The East can sleep very well but cannot be active. In the morning the Eastern mind also feels lethargic, sleepy. For centuries they have been sleeping well but not doing anything else. Now the West has done much, but now you have created an unease, a *dis*-ease. And because of that *dis*-ease, everything is useless, whatsoever you have done is useless. You cannot even sleep honestly!

## Balancing the Rational and the Irrational

So this is why my emphasis is always to train the mind for activity, at the same time for inactivity, and thirdly, the most significant, trained for the movement – so you can move and the mind can be trained. You can move, I can move, from any activity, in a single moment to inactivity. I can move: I can talk with you for hours and then I can move in a single moment to an inner, deep silence with no talk, going in. Unless this is created you have stunted growth.

So to me the future has to be a deep harmony between inner polarities. Unless this movement is created human query is exhausted. You cannot go on. You cannot go further. The East is exhausted; the West is exhausted. You can change but then, within two centuries, again the same problem comes on. Then we begin to move in a circle.

*I am fascinated by your dialectic view of human history but I don't quite follow when you see that complete dichotomy between rational thought and irrational thought.*
*Look at traditional society. In both the West and the East the normal picture would be that there were plenty of scientists and people who were, in their professional work, active in the rational pursuit of thinking, who at the same time were deeply religious people and active in this irrational aspect, operating on two different planes and not necessarily harming one another. And there could be, and sometimes was, the kind of harmony or interplay between the two sides which you have talked about so eloquently. I don't think it's really the rational thinking which got us into trouble. I think it's the application of the result of our rational thinking. It's the goal of our society, the image of*

*"progress," which is very much what the young people do not accept anymore, and I think they may be right there. But I would not equate that with rational thinking. I would rather think that there is a mistake somewhere along the line. The goals of our society have become so deformed...*

**I understand, I understand.** But really, the very search for goals is part of the rational process. Really, the future exists for reason. That's why for animals there is no future and there is no goal. They live, but there is no goal. Reason creates the ideals, reason creates the goals, reason creates the future. So the real problem is not whether to have right goals or wrong goals. The real question is whether to have goals or not.

The new generation is asking whether to have goals or not. The moment you have a goal, you begin to distort life because then you begin to mold it according to the goal. Then the present becomes less meaningful. The future takes the meaning and the present has to be molded, adjusted with the future.

So this goal-oriented mind is the reason, and the life-oriented mind is the irreason.

*On one hand you say that all human potentialities have to be realized, and that one is practically as good as the other, and the more we press anything we create an imbalance and trouble. At the same time you are also talking about the hippies, you say that they are behaving like children, or they are in a state of regression, if I have understood rightly. So you have a certain image of what the human being should be like, a specific goal.*

## Balancing the Rational and the Irrational

**I have – what I am saying...** I have: what I am saying is that it is not a question of reason having the "right" goals. The question is of reason not being the alone phenomena, the lonely phenomena of the human mind.

Reason has to have goals; reason cannot exist without goals. But this must not become dictatorial. So reason has to have goals. It cannot work, reason cannot work without the space created by the future. Reason cannot work without a goal somewhere, to reach, to be reached. Reason has to work with goals, but reason must not be the dominant thing. It must not be dictatorial. It must not be the only branch growing.

What I am saying is reason has to have goals; it cannot exist without them, and reason must exist, it is a potentiality. Then there is the anti-reason part of the human mind which cannot have goals, which is just like animals, just like children. Just like children it can only exist here and now. And really it is that part which experiences the deeper realms of life, of love, of beauty, of art. That part, that irrational part, experiences the deeper realms, because it can go deep in the present. It has no need to go into the future. It can go deep just here and now, in this very moment. This part must be grown simultaneously, and you can do this in two ways.

You said rightly, there have been scientists with a very deep religious personality, but as I see it, this can be done in two ways. Either it can be a deep harmony, or it can just be a closing of one aperture and an opening of another, without any harmony. Without any harmony, I can be a scientist and then I can close my scientific world and I can go to a church and pray. Then the scientist is not praying there, then the scientist is not praying – the scientist has been left out. It is not really a harmony. It is just a deep bifurcation.

There is no harmony, there is no inner dialogue between the scientist and the worshipper. There is no dialogue. The scientist has not come to the church at all. And when this man goes to his lab, the worshipper is left out; it has not come in.

So this is really a deep division and a closed division. They don't overlap. They don't overlap, so in such a person you will feel a dichotomy, not a harmony, not a harmony. He will be saying things which he himself will feel guilty to have said. He will be making statements as a scientist which go quite against his mind as a worshipper, and he cannot make any harmonious whole within the two.

So many scientists have really lived very schizophrenic lives. One part of them is something, and another part is something else. This is not what I mean by harmony. By harmony I mean with no closing. You are capable of moving – with no closing. The scientist goes to pray and the religious man comes to the lab. There is no division. There is no gap.

Otherwise, you can have two persons inside, you can have many. You can have many – and we do ordinarily. We have multi-personalities, and we become identified with one. Then we move into a different gear, then we change the gear, we become something else. This gear changing is there. This is not really a harmony, and this will create a very deep tension in your being because you cannot be at ease with so many divisions.

An undivided consciousness, capable of movement to the polar opposite, is possible only when we have a total conception of the human being as intrinsically *with* opposites – naturally with opposites, no denial of the opposites. For example, if I go to pray I won't feel any tension about

## Balancing the Rational and the Irrational

it – then what am I doing? Is it logical? Is it rational? Is there any God?

If I work in the lab then doubt works. Can I conceive of my being with doubt as an instrument of worth, not as a fixation? Faith is also an instrument of worth. They are just two aspects, to look into different dimensions. So when you have to see far you change your aspect; nearer you change your aspect. You are not faced with your aspects, no fixation, and there is no inherent dichotomy felt. The person must not feel any dichotomy, any division, and must easily, smoothly move. Even the movement should not be felt. And when there is really a deep harmony the movement is not felt. You move, but the movement is not felt because movement is only felt against obstacles.

And one thing more. I know when I say "East" and "West" I don't mean that in the West there have been no Eastern minds, and I don't mean that in the East there have been no Western minds. Really the East and the West is less geographical, more psychological. There are minds in the West who are Eastern and there are minds in the East who are Western. But the main current – I am talking about the main current.

For example, an Eckhart or Bonheim; they belong to the East. They belong to the East; they must not be included in the history of the West. They belong to the East. And really sometime we must have a psychological history of the world in which the East will have many faces from the West, and the West will have many faces from the East, and many names. Whatsoever we have been doing is geographical history. We must conceive of a psychological history – a more developed form of history in which the world is divided not geographically, but psychologically.

So I don't mean that they are not, but the main current, the main current in the West has been a rational growth, even religiously also. That's why the church became so dominant. Hinduism really has no church, or a very anarchic phenomenon – because with an irrational religion how can you have a theology, argumentative, with proof of God, and a church, and a representative, a pope? You cannot have it.

Even in the West religion developed through the lines of reason. Jesus himself is an irrational man, but Saint Paul is not. Saint Paul had a very scientific mind, very scientific, very rational. So really Christianity belongs to Saint Paul, not to Jesus at all. With Jesus there can be no Christianity. It is impossible. Such an anarchic man, no possibility of such a big organization, such a big kingdom. He was talking of something else when he was talking about kingdoms. But such a big kingdom of the church – just "churchdom" – is impossible with Jesus. He was Eastern, but Saint Paul was not.

So even the church has gone, and that's why there was a conflict between science and church, because both were rational. And both were trying to rationalize a phenomenon. The church had to be defeated, because it could not be so rational, because its center was religion. The church tried to be rational but it could not be, because the phenomenon itself was irrational. Reason is something foreign to religion; that's why the church had to go down and science could win.

But in the East there is no fight between science and religion because religion has never claimed any reason, so there is no fight. They don't belong to the same realm at all. The whole progress has been Aristotelian; Aristotle remains yet the center of the West.

## Balancing the Rational and the Irrational

*What is the point of the quest of the human individual, of the image of the human being both in the East and in the West, and in religious thought as well as in atheist philosophy? All of these always had a certain ideal image of a human being, of his potentialities which should be developed, realized, which always included a certain preference for certain features of the human being, in contrast to what you said. And now whether you do that by repression or by sublimation or by some other process, makes no difference. But basically the idea always is that the human image is something greater than I am and toward which I must trial. How do you reconcile this with the image of a human being whose potentialities all have equal value – the positive and the negative, or the animal and the non-animal, etcetera, etcetera?*

**This strange phenomena happens** not because of religion, but whenever religion has to be systematized, this phenomena happens. For example, a Buddha is not after any ideal. A Buddha himself is not after any ideal, or a Jesus himself is not after any ideal. They live very spontaneous lives, but they become ideals – *they* become ideals. They live very spontaneous lives and they grow in their own way, whatsoever way and whatsoever ultimate shape the pattern takes. They grow, they grow like a wild tree, but for the followers that wild tree becomes an ideal. And then the followers begin to have patterns, preferences, choices, condemnations.

So really religion has two parts. One, a deeply religious personality, is a phenomena, a spontaneous phenomena. It happens, and the followers who create the creed, who create the dogmas, who create the disciplines, they create according to the ideal. Then a Buddhist has an ideal – "One must be like Buddha." Then preferences have to be met because Buddha was never seen to be angry. It may have been a spontaneous growth for him, but then the follower must not be angry; it becomes a "must not." Then you have to suppress or sublimate, or howsoever you name it, it means the same. Then you have to destroy yourself in many ways, because only then you can create the image. Then you have to become an imitation.

And to me, this is criminal. A religious personality is a beautiful phenomena, but a religious creed is a rationalized thing again. This is reason coming in and encountering a non-rational phenomenon.

*Buddha incidentally was a very rational person...*

**He was very rational,** but with very irrational gaps. And he was very at ease with irrational gaps also. And the concept of Buddha that we have is not really of the Buddha, but the rationalist tradition that followed and created the whole concept.

Really, to encounter Buddha is a different thing. But we cannot do otherwise. We have to go through the Buddhists, a long tradition of two thousand years, and they have created, they have made him very rational. He was not so. Really you cannot be if you are deep in existence. You cannot be. You have to be many times very irrational – and a Buddha is. But then we have to put aside the whole tradition and go directly. It is difficult, very difficult.

## Balancing the Rational and the Irrational

*We can never meet a Buddha or a Lao Tzu, the direct meeting is impossible.*

**It is impossible in a way,** but we can make some effort and that effort pays; that effort is paying. New realms become – you have new glimpses. Because, for example – this happens, this is daily happening – if I am talking to a rational person, he chooses. He leaves all that even unconsciously was not rational. And if I am talking with a poet he chooses something else. When I talk to a rational man even the same sentence, the same words, signify something else, because he cannot look at the poetry of the words. He can only look at the logic, at the argument of the words. That argument has a different dimension. A poet, a painter, can have a different dimension of the word. The word has a shade, a color. The word has a rhythm, a poetry. This is not at all connected with argument.

So Buddha – the faces of Buddha we must say, not face – the faces of Buddha are different, are different. They are according to the person who has seen him. And in India, the Buddhist phenomena happened in such a period when the whole country was going through a rational crisis. It was going against the irrational; a crisis of the whole irrational Vedas, Upanishads, of the whole mysticism – it was going against it. The movement was such that the whole mind of the country, and particularly of Bihar, was concerned...was against mysticism.

And Buddha was charismatic, and Buddha was hypnotic. People were impressed by him. But the interpretation of the Buddhist face is bound to be rational – is bound to be. Buddha happening in another part of history, in a world that was not against mysticism, would have been taken as a great mystic, not as a great intellectual. So it happens. It happens that the face belongs to the history of a particular time.

But as I see it, Buddha is not, he cannot be. The whole concept of nirvana is just mystical, and he is even more mystical than the Upanishads, because the Upanishads, howsoever mystical they will look, they have their own rationality. They talk about transmigration, but they talk about transmigration with a soul. It is rational. Buddha talks about transmigration without a soul. It is more mystical. It is more mystical – transmigration without a soul. The Upanishads talk about liberation, but *you* will be there. This is rational, otherwise the whole thing becomes nonsense. If I cannot be in that ultimate state of existence, then the whole effort is useless, illogical. Buddha says the effort has to be made – and then you will not be there; it will be just nothingness.

It is more mystical.

*Coming back to the hippies, when you say that they are regressing, they are behaving like children, or they are behaving like savages, I quite agree with you. But in saying this do you not judge, compare their behavior to a different kind of behavior, to a superior kind of behavior? So you do have an image there which you might call an ideal image.*

**Not really an image,** not really an image, but a different thing. When I say they are behaving like children, I mean they are not growing. Regressing. I don't have any image that they should confirm. I have a concept of growth, not of image, not of image. I don't want that they should be attuned,

## Balancing the Rational and the Irrational

adjusted, to a particular image. What I am saying is only that they are regressing into the past, not growing into the future. I have no image of the tree that is to grow – but it must grow without any image. It must not regress. So it is a question of growth and regression, not of any image.

Secondly, when I say they are regressing, I mean they are reacting against a too rational society. They are reacting, but the reaction is going to the other extreme, with the same fallacy. Reason must be absorbed, must not be left out. If you leave it out, then you are doing the same, the same error that left the irreason out.

The Victorian culture created a man like a facade, like a face. Not as a living being inside, but a pattern of behavior, a pattern of mannerisms – a face more and a being less. That was possible because we chose only reason to be the criterion of everything. So the irrational, the anarchic, the chaotic inside, was pushed out, suppressed. Now that the anarchic side is taking revenge, it can do two things. It can be destructive, then it will be regressive.

If it is destructive then it will take revenge on the same coin. It will deny the rational part. It will deny the rational part, and then you become just like children, immature. You fall down.

If it is to be creative, it must not commit the same error. It must absorb the reason with the irrational. It must absorb both. Then it will be growing, growing in comparison to both – the one who has denied the irrational and the one who has denied the rational. They are both not growing.

They are both not growing because you cannot grow unless you grow totally. There is no growth unless you grow totally. So I have no image to compare to.

*One small question. In the West we've especially been very formed or deformed by the concept of sin and the concept of guilt. They are concepts which are absent as you know in the East. Consequently the young people here in the East do not have the same kind of problems. In which way is that reflected amongst your followers? Are there really different needs, and different problems between your Western followers and your Eastern followers?*

**Yes, bound to be, bound to be,** because the concept of sin creates a very different consciousness around it. The same concept is lacking in the Eastern mind. Rather, it is substituted by the concept of ignorance. In the Eastern consciousness, the root of all evil is ignorance not sin. The root is because you are ignorant. So the problem is not of guilt but of discipline. You have to be more aware, more knowing. So in the East, knowledge is transformation – so meditation becomes the source, the very instrument.

In the West with Christianity, sin became the center. It is not because you are ignorant that you commit sin. You sin; that's why you are ignorant. The sin takes a primary significance – and not only is it your sin, it is the original sin of humanity. So you are burdened with a concept of sin. It creates guilt, it creates tension. That's why Christianity could really not develop meditative techniques. It developed only prayer – because against sin what can you do? You can be moral and prayerful.

So really nothing exists in the East like the Ten Commandments. Nothing exists like that in the East; there is not a too-moralistic concept there, so the problems are different. From the West, for people coming from the West,

## Balancing the Rational and the Irrational

guilt is their problem. Deep down they feel guilty. Even those who have revolted, deep down they feel guilt. So it is more a psychological problem, concerned with the mind and less concerned with the being.

So their guilt has to be released. That's why the West had to develop psychoanalysis, or confession. They were not developed in the East because they were never needed. You have to confess, only then can you be free from the guilt deep down. Or you have to go through psychoanalysis, a long process of thought association, so the guilt is thrown out. But it is never thrown out permanently. It will come again because the concept of sin remains. It will be created again; it will accumulate again.

So psychoanalysis can only be a temporary help, and confession is also a temporary help. You have to confess again and again. These are temporary helps against something that has been accepted; the root of the disease has been accepted.

In the East, it is not a question of psychology. It is a question of being. So it is not a question of mental health. Rather, it is a question of spiritual growth. You have to grow spiritually, to be more aware of things. You have not to change your basic behavior, but to change your basic consciousness. Then the behavior follows.

So Christianity is more behavioristic, and in that way it is defective, because behavior is just the periphery. The question is not of what you do; the question is of what you are. So if you go on changing your doings, you are not changing. And you can remain the same in a quite contrary doing. You can be a saint and still with the same being, because doing can be changed very easily. It can be forced.

So whosoever is coming from the West, their problem is

of behavior, guilt. And I struggle with them just to make them aware of a deeper problem – which is of being, not of the psyche.

> *Behavior is also important in the Buddhist world. Behavior, ethical behavior, is very important, very much like in Christianity, without a feeling of guilt. There is a lot of emphasis on it, but not in Hindu thought.* That's true, you're right.

**Yes, in Buddhism** – and in Jainism – it is too much, but without the concept of sin, without the concept of sin. It is too much. But they have also created – not the same guilt feeling – but in a different way they have created it. Particularly Jainas have created a very deep inferiority. Guilt is not there because there is no question of sin, but a deep inferiority complex, that a person is inferior. Unless one goes beyond all the sins, one cannot be superior, one cannot be superior. A very deep inferiority is there, and this deep inferiority works in the same way. It creates problems.

That's why Jainas have not created any meditative techniques. They have created only ethical formulas: do this, do this, don't do that. And the whole concept is centered around the behavior. That's why Jainism has become just a dead thing. You go to a Jaina monk; he is an ideal as far as behavior is concerned, but as far as the inner being is concerned he is poor – just poor with no inner being. He goes on behaving just like a puppet.

So Jainism is dead. Buddhism is not dead in the same way because a different emphasis is there. In Buddhism a

## Balancing the Rational and the Irrational

different emphasis is there. The ethical part of Buddha is just a consequence of the meditative part, and if behavior has to be changed, it is just a part of meditation. It is just a part of meditation, as a help to meditation. In itself, it is meaningless. In itself, it is meaningless. In Christianity, it is meaningful in itself; in Jainism, it is meaningful in itself. If you are doing good, then you are good. For Buddha it is not the case. You have to be transformed inwardly. Doing good can help it, can become a part, can become a part, can become a part, but meditation is the center.

So only Buddhists have developed deep meditations. Deep meditations. Everything else is just a help – not significant. You can even discard it. It remains on your strength. The question is of your strength; you can discard it. If you can meditate without the help, then you can discard it.

But Hinduism is still more complex and deeper, deeper. That's why Hinduism could develop a different dimension of Tantra, so that whatsoever you call sin, even that can be used. Hinduism is in a way very healthy – chaotic, of course, because anything healthy is bound to be chaotic, bound to be. It cannot be systematized. It cannot be systematized.

## About the Author

Osho defies categorization. His thousands of talks cover everything from the individual quest for meaning to the most urgent social and political issues facing society today. Osho's books are not written but are transcribed from audio and video recordings of his extemporaneous talks to international audiences. As he puts it, "So remember: whatever I am saying is not just for you... I am talking also for the future generations."

Osho has been described by *The Sunday Times* in London as one of the "1000 Makers of the 20th Century" and by American author Tom Robbins as "the most dangerous man since Jesus Christ." *Sunday Mid-Day* (India) has selected Osho as one of ten people – along with Gandhi, Nehru and

Buddha – who have changed the destiny of India.

About his own work Osho has said that he is helping to create the conditions for the birth of a new kind of human being. He often characterizes this new human being as "Zorba the Buddha" – capable both of enjoying the earthy pleasures of a Zorba the Greek and the silent serenity of a Gautama the Buddha.

Running like a thread through all aspects of Osho's talks and meditations is a vision that encompasses both the timeless wisdom of all ages past and the highest potential of today's (and tomorrow's) science and technology.

Osho is known for his revolutionary contribution to the science of inner transformation, with an approach to meditation that acknowledges the accelerated pace of contemporary life. His unique OSHO Active Meditations are designed to first release the accumulated stresses of body and mind, so that it is then easier to take an experience of stillness and thought-free relaxation into daily life.

Two autobiographical works by the author are available:

***Autobiography of a Spiritually Incorrect Mystic,***
St Martins Press, USA
***Glimpses of a Golden Childhood,***
OSHO Media International, Pune, India

*OSHO International Meditation Resort*

**Location**
Located 100 miles southeast of Mumbai in the thriving modern city of Pune, India, the OSHO International Meditation Resort is a holiday destination with a difference. The Meditation Resort is spread over 28 acres of spectacular gardens in a beautiful tree-lined residential area.

**Uniqueness**
Each year the Meditation Resort welcomes thousands of people from more than 100 countries. The unique campus provides an opportunity for a direct personal experience of a new way of living – with more awareness, relaxation, celebration and creativity. A great variety of around-the-clock and

around-the-year program options are available. Doing nothing and just relaxing is one of them!

All programs are based on the OSHO vision of "Zorba the Buddha" – a qualitatively new kind of human being who is able *both* to participate creatively in everyday life *and* to relax into silence and meditation.

## THE DETAILS
### Meditations
A full daily schedule of meditations for every type of person includes methods that are active and passive, traditional and revolutionary, and in particular the OSHO Active Meditations™. The meditations take place in what must be the world's largest meditation hall, the Osho Auditorium.

### Multiversity
Individual sessions, courses and workshops cover everything from creative arts to holistic health, personal transformation, relationship and life transition, work-as-meditation, esoteric sciences, and the "Zen" approach to sports and recreation. The secret of the Multiversity's success lies in the fact that all its programs are combined with meditation, supporting the understanding that as human beings we are far more than the sum of our parts.

**Basho Spa**
The luxurious Basho Spa provides for leisurely open-air swimming surrounded by trees and tropical green. The uniquely styled, spacious Jacuzzi, the saunas, gym, tennis courts … all these are enhanced by their stunningly beautiful setting.

**Cuisine**
A variety of different eating areas serve delicious Western, Asian and Indian vegetarian food – most of it organically grown especially for the Meditation Resort. Breads and cakes are baked in the resort's own bakery.

**Night life**
There are many evening events to choose from – dancing being at the top of the list! Other activities include full-moon meditations beneath the stars, variety shows, music performances and meditations for daily life.
Or you can just enjoy meeting people at the Plaza Café, or walking in the nighttime serenity of the gardens of this fairytale environment.

**Facilities**
You can buy all your basic necessities and toiletries in the Galleria. The Multimedia Gallery

sells a large range of OSHO media products. There is also a bank, a travel agency and a Cyber Café on-campus. For those who enjoy shopping, Pune provides all the options, ranging from traditional and ethnic Indian products to all of the global brand-name stores.

**Accommodation**

You can choose to stay in the elegant rooms of the Osho Guesthouse, or for longer stays opt for one of the Living-In program packages. Additionally there is a plentiful variety of nearby hotels and serviced apartments.

www.osho.com/meditationresort
www.osho.com/guesthouse
www.osho.com/livingin

*More OSHO Books*

### Above All, Don't Wobble
*Individual Meetings with a Contemporary Mystic*
An extraordinary chronicle of meetings between the contemporary mystic, Osho, and people of all ages and all walks of life, from around the world.

People who have participated in some of the self discovery and meditations programs offered around Osho have an opportunity to ask personal questions or share their experiences. In these humorous, unpredictable, one-off dialogues, Osho responds very personally to each individual with unique insights and support.

ISBN 978-81-7261-202-3


### Vedanta: Seven Steps to Samadhi
*Talks on the Akshyupanishad*
These series of talks in this book were given by Osho during a nine day meditation retreat on Mount Abu, in India, to hundreds of seekers gathered to hear about and experiment with his revolutionary meditation techniques.

Each day Osho comments on verses from the Aksyupanishad and its "seven steps to Samadhi," bringing contemporary relevance to the 5000-year-old teachings and making them accessible to seekers from both East and West.

ISBN 978-81-7261-012-8

**Beyond Psychology**
*Talks in Uruguay*

In this book Osho shows us that the real meaning of "taking responsibility" is to go beyond the narrow confines of the mind. Showing us why psychological answers to our self-made miseries will never work, Osho gives many techniques to help us step beyond our psychology. He answers our most personal and existential questions, and takes a radical new look at a variety of esoteric subjects.

ISBN 978-81-7261-195-8


**The Book of Secrets**
*112 Keys to the Mystery Within*

In *The Book of Secrets* we are invited to experience and experiment with the games and situations that everyday life brings through the tools of our senses. The 4000-year-old Vigyan Bhairav Tantra is a compendium of highly condensed, telegraphic instructions for 112 different awareness techniques that bring us into the present moment. Osho describes each technique in detail, and explains how we can discover which is the best one for us and how to integrate it into our daily lives.

"These techniques, if followed, suddenly turn your mind. It comes to the present. And when the mind comes to the present it stops, it is no more. You cannot be a mind in the present, that is impossible."
Osho

ISBN 978-81-7261-217-7

### The Secret of Secrets
*Talks on The Secret of the Golden Flower*

Osho describes The Secret of the Golden Flower as very ancient and: "…one of the most esoteric treatises in the world. It will show you the way to become more than the body. It will show you the way to go beyond death."

He gives specific instructions for the Taoist Golden Light Meditation which helps harmonize the male and female elements and transmute sexual energy.

He also answers related questions covering subjects as diverse as the difference between male and female energies, sex, fear, aloneness, the differences and similarities between Tao, Yoga, and Tantra, the significance of the third eye, and how to become integrated through watching.

ISBN 978-81-7261-106-4

*For More Information*

Thanks for buying this OSHO book.

It wasn't long ago when websites were the sole source of all information and social networking sites were considered vehicles for teens and college kids to interact with each other and share personal interests. Times have changed, and so have we.

You can now find more OSHO unique content in multiple languages and formats at the following websites online:

Official website of OSHO International @ www.OSHO.com

You can search the open access OSHO library for your favorite topic @ www.OSHO.com/Library

A complete presentation of all the OSHO meditations and related music can be found @ www.OSHO.com/Meditation

To plan a visit to OSHO International Meditation Resort you can visit @ www.OSHO.com/MeditationResort

Latest updates about events, festivals, media releases and quotes are updated daily @ www.facebook.com/OSHO.International

All latest happenings, including information about the OSHO Multiversity courses, are updated daily @ www.facebook.com/OSHO.International.Meditation.Resort

You can wake up to a daily OSHO quote @ www.twitter.com/OSHOtimes

Your instant access to OSHO video channel can be found @ www.youtube.com/OSHO International

To make OSHO available in your local language you can register and transcribe or translate OSHO Talks @ www.OSHOtalks.info

Please take a moment to **register and browse** these sites as they provide much more information about OSHO.
You may also discover many fun and exciting ways to **get involved** in making OSHO available around the world.

Happy reading.